Where Cotton Grows

Mike Reed

Bloomington, IN Milton Keynes, UK
authorHOUSE®

AuthorHouse™
1663 Liberty Drive, Suite 200
Bloomington, IN 47403
www.authorhouse.com
Phone: 1-800-839-8640

AuthorHouse™ UK Ltd.
500 Avebury Boulevard
Central Milton Keynes, MK9 2BE
www.authorhouse.co.uk
Phone: 08001974150

This book is a work of fiction. People, places, events, and situations are the product of the author's imagination. Any resemblance to actual persons, living or dead, or historical events, is purely coincidental.

© 2006 Mike Reed. All rights reserved.

No part of this book may be reproduced, stored in a retrieval system, or transmitted by any means without the written permission of the author.

First published by AuthorHouse 11/27/2006

ISBN: 978-1-4259-7984-3 (sc)
ISBN: 978-1-4259-7983-6 (hc)

Printed in the United States of America
Bloomington, Indiana

This book is printed on acid-free paper.

Dedication

I dedicate this book to my wife Kay, who for thirty four years has followed me through a career in the military and waited patiently for my return while I worked as a civilian contractor in the Middle East. To our children, Becky, Bobby and our son-in-law, Jacob; thank you for all the happiness you have given us. To the memory of my Mother and Father, who through long years of suffering, never failed to give the one thing valued most in a child's life, love.

Life just isn't fair! You're born, you try your best to find your niche in life, you work, and then you die. For some, life offers a bit more phosphorous fruit, but by and large, being born in a small Mississippi town, never really produced great odds for success to those who experienced it. In my town, you could count on your hands those who were successful, usually at the expense of those with whom they came in contact. It has been said that there were so many bootleggers they often had to tie a red scarf around their arm when attending county affairs to keep from selling to each other! Personally, I could not confirm nor deny this; however, I do know that "old John Barleycorn" most assuredly enjoyed a profound presence.

When I was just a young boy, I would sit for hours listening to my Grandfather tell stories of how life once was in the small, out of the way, hamlet of Greensboro, Mississippi. Though there was never a lot to do, an inventive imagination could render just enough for trouble to find you, and usually it did. Regardless of how hard we tried, trouble always seemed to find its way.

People in Greensboro were friendly, outgoing, hard-working and usually very interested in everyone else's business. The best news distributed usually could be learned on Main Street on Saturday afternoons, where masses would congregate to purchase weekly supplies for the week that lay ahead on the farm. People only came to town once a week, so it was a day of relaxation, loud talking, gossip, and renewing old acquaintances. But, by and large, mostly gossip. It was on a Saturday, in early summer that I learned what having a baby out of wedlock was. Until then, my only experience concerned mostly the birth of livestock. In our town, there were two defined areas of living, Greensboro, and "the hill". The hill, located within Greensboro itself, was located just east, separated only by a creek. The "colored" people occupied the hill, while the whites occupied Greensboro. Though we all lived peacefully in our respective locations, there were times when those of affluence would "visit" the hill, and spend time of a personal nature there. Talk was rampant, but somehow overlooked and it continued well into the nineteen sixties and nineteen seventies. Four young high school boys, in their early teens, embarked upon a path that would change their otherwise dull existences. They had no idea that what they would experience on this day would profoundly change their lives forever, and cause them to grow and move beyond the small town life they had grown to know and love so dearly.

The creek which separated Greensboro and 'the hill' was a well known place to rid oneself of the summer heat, so most energetic teenagers would congregate there at a favorite spot, commonly referred to as "the hole", and rid themselves of their attire, and either wade or dive into the cool waters of Dunn Creek. Usually, the swimming parties were not of a coed nature, but from time to time, those from 'the hill', would also come to the creek and enjoy the coolness of the midday waters, to wash off the heat and accumulation of dust. Myra Burns, a young black girl, in her mid teens, but considered among those in Greensboro to be half white, also swam in the creek. Myra, who was very pretty, and for her age, a very developed young lady? Her features were those of Caucasian, with fine hair, slim lined nose, European facial features, and not that of African descent. Myra, who had quit school, to work in the local, back alley café, ran by her father, was considered and accepted by both Greensboro and "the hill".

The four young teenagers, stripped themselves of their clothes, and waded deep into the waters of Dunn Creek, splashing water, ducking each other, and swinging from vines that hung low and just above the hole. It was a day of leisure, and no one was going to rob them of this opportunity to have fun. As they swam, they heard the voices of girls coming from nearby bushes. Of course, being boys, what did it matter, they were well submerged beneath the cold waters of Dunn Creek. All of a sudden, Myra, with a girlish voice, stuck her head out from behind the bushes and laughed, remarking about the "short-comings" of the boys. Exchanging words and growing in some degree of comfort, the boys invited Myra and her friends into the cool waters. After deliberation, the girls, accepted the offer, but asked the boys to turn their backs, and told them they would come in, but the boys would have to remain in their part of the creek, while they, the girls, would swim in a spot just up from them. An agreement was reached, and the girls disrobed and waded in. As the evening progressed, the Sun lowered, and the girls who accompanied Myra, one by one, opted to return to their chores and household duties, with exception of Myra. Having grown to know and trust the young boys, Myra, who was a little more than a year older than the oldest boy, decided to stay and swim with her new-found white friends. The boys, male hormones raging, played games, and at every opportunity, tried to get as close to Myra as they could, hoping to just rub past her, in hopes of getting close enough to possibly "feel" the femininity of this young girl, who was very well proportioned. As games persisted, laughter grew, touches were made, and Myra, before she knew it, allowed herself to be touched by all of the boys. She liked it, because in Greensboro, for a black girl to feel the touch of a white boy, was just never something that happened. Besides, in her thinking, it was harmless, and these were just boys. Her new-found friends and she had a place to come, be on a even accord, and just be teenagers. Finally, Myra, realizing the day had escaped her, hurriedly left the hole and the four young boys, who were angered from the fact, that they got no place, with exception of "rubbing" past the soft exposed body of a teenage girl, and feeling what they thought might have been a breast. It was not a good day, but there was always tomorrow.

    Myra made her way to the backstreet café where her father would meet her with a stern look and anger in his eyes. He questioned her as to where she was the day prior, when she was supposed to have been helping her mother with household chores. As she attempted to explain, he slapped her face, scolded her to never go near the creek again, telling her that if she did she would live to regret her desire for being with her friends. Myra cried, wiped her tears, turned and ran back down the street, making her way through the crooked streets of Greensboro on her way home. When she arrived at her doorstep, her Mother met her asking, "Myra, what's wrong?" Myra answered by saying she had run into some bushes, hitting her face, and that it hurt. Her Mother quickly took her inside, washed her face, and put some ointment on it in hopes of making her feel better. "There, that should do it, honey". "You need to be more careful, and watch where you are going." "I will, Mama", said Myra.

    "Myra!" The call rang from the back room of the house. "Yes, Mama", replied Myra. "Can you please come and help me?" As Myra entered the back room, a place where her Mama sewed and took in laundry, Myra took a seat, in an old cane bottomed chair, where she could look and talk with her Mother. Her mother said, "Myra, did your Daddy hit you?" "Yes", replied Myra. "What on earth for?" Myra's head dropped, and again with tears in her eyes, she explained to her Mother about her new found friends at the swimming hole. "Honey, we folks have no place with them folks. You ought to know that." Myra exclaimed, "I know, Mama, but they are nice boys, and they like me." Myra's mother replied, "Myra, no white boy likes a colored girl, simply for the sake of just liking her. They have other things on their minds, and for you those other things aren't good." "Like what, Mama?" Myra's Mother, with a look of desperation in her eyes, now had to explain to her daughter.

The next day Myra sat quietly on the front porch, shelling peas, as had been instructed by her Mother. When she finished, she noticed her friend, May belle, playing in her front yard, jumping rope. "May belle", called Myra, whatcha doing?" "Just playing, what about you?" "Finished my chores, and wishing I had something to do", replied Myra. "Wanna go to the hole", said May belle? "Yep, but I can't, I'll get whipped", replied Myra. "Oh! Myra, it ain;t fair, we got nothing to do, and it's such a pretty day." The girls talked back and forth, discussing how they could go swim, and not get caught.

As the girls made their way down the crooked path to the creek, voices could be heard coming from the hole. As they cautiously approached, Myra, smiled, as she saw her friends once again in the hole, splashing, and ducking one another. As the girls took off their clothes, and eased into the water, just beyond a small bend in the creek, the boys noticed their presence and began to splash water on the girls. The girls splashed back, and before long, a water war was on, and laughter was teeming. After a while, as the activity slowed down, the teenagers began to talk. They made bets of daring back and forth, and before you know it, they were jumping from limbs high in the trees down into the cold waters of Dunn Creek.

The boy, who Myra thought was the nicest, was Tommy Fowler. Tommy's father was a businessman in town, highly respected, and active in the First Baptist Church. Tommy thought Myra was pretty, and Myra caught his eye from time to time, as he looked upon her sitting there on the bank, with no cover on at all. Tommy came and sat by Myra. He told her that he thought she was a nice girl, and very pretty. Holding her hand, rubbing her milky skin so soft, he turned his face toward hers and kissed her. Not knowing what it would be like to kiss a colored girl, he became shocked. Myra's kiss was warm and exciting. Her skin was warm and pleasant to his touch. Myra enjoyed Tommy's kiss. She had never kissed a white boy. Although it was exciting to her, it was also a scary feeling. What if anyone had seen them? Surely she would be beaten and ridiculed. She was colored, and whites and coloreds did not do such as this. One thing Myra did know. When Tommy's lips touched her, she didn't feel color, she felt her heart skip beats, and she tingled all over. Tommy. Confessing to her that he liked her lot, Tommy felt in his heart the same feeling. Both were afraid but not sorry for what they had done. He liked the feeling of Myra in his arms. He felt no shame for having told her she was pretty and for kissing her. She was a beautiful young woman. He felt lucky. He ached as he thought; he had to keep his secret with this beautiful young woman deep inside his heart. He could never tell anyone, yet he knew already that he loved her. It was a love that would always be felt but never united. The others were still playing, splashing and ducking, acting like the teenagers they were, but Tommy, in a subtle way had begun to notice Myra and her Womanhood. Tommy asked Myra if she had a boyfriend and she replied, "No". He asked "Why not, you're so pretty?" As Myra blushed and smiled, turning her head, she replied, "I'm colored, and not many people notice me." Tommy put his hand on Myra's hand, holding it, and telling her he thought she was so pretty. Myra, having never heard this before, did not know how to respond, especially since it was coming from a white boy. As they sat and talked, the others having forgotten about Myra and Tommy, sitting just beyond the bend, on the banks naked got dressed and walked back to town, leaving Tommy and Myra to the conversation. As Tommy kissed Myra, she felt warmth so unlike anything she had ever felt before, and within a short time, Tommy and Myra were lying on the banks engaging in an act unacceptable by biblical belief, not to mention the feelings of the townspeople.

Myra walked up to her front porch, singing and with a smile on her face. Her Mother looked at her, rather concerned, as Myra, just prior, was exhibiting a depressed mood. Myra's Mother asked, "Child, what on earth?" Myra explained, she had been with her friend, and they had just walked.

~ ~ ~

The summer grew long and hot, and so did tensions in the local election. The colored populous did not vote, as they were not permitted too. The Democrats promised better days, a better life, and more jobs, while the colored felt in their hearts, worse days, poorer life, and fewer jobs, if any, which meant, more scrapping by would take place.

It was in the fall when Myra became ill. She would awaken, try to eat, get sick, vomit, and start her day. She made her way to and from her Father's place of work, helping him in the café, waiting tables, and cleaning. The white merchants, from time to time, would visit the café to indulge in some of her Fathers' delicious home cooked food. He was an Old South cook, specializing in purple hull peas, okra, skillet fried corn, cornbread, fresh onions, lettuce, sweetened iced tea, and homemade apple and peach cobblers. A meal from his café would leave one full for a solid day, mainly due to the amount of grease used in cooking each meal. It kind of lay heavy on the stomach, and would either result in a frequent trip to the bathroom, or an upset stomach, but his food was good. You just had to allow your stomach time to get accustomed.

Myra's Mother had begun to notice her daughter's signs of illness. She at first passed it off as the "bug", but as time passed, and it continued, she approached Myra one night as they were cleaning the kitchen. Myra's Mother asked if she wanted to discuss anything with her. "No Mam", said Myra. "Well, honey, as a Mama, I can tell you one thing for sure: I know you better than you know yourself, and, young lady, you are pregnant!" Myra, just looking at her Mother, felt as cold as the March winds inside of herself. "Mama, I can't be!" "Honey, I have had seven children, and I know: What on earth are we going to tell your Daddy? Who is the Daddy? Is it the boy at the Café, who cooks with your Daddy? He's been eyeing you now for some time. As Myra, confided in her Mother, she told her about her young friend from the creek. Her Mother shouted, "Oh! Lord!", and began to cry. "He will kill you honey! He will kill you."

As the days passed, then months, Myra's clothes were loosened to allow her body room to look as if she was gaining weight, but naturally. Both she and her Mother knew the day would come that the secret no longer could be kept, thus revealing the fear she had come to dread. The local doctor, a man of kindness and good hearted ways, had begun to see Myra. He, as well as her Mother did everything to keep the secret. The doctor, being the kind man he was, had suggested that if Myra wished, he would deliver the baby, and offer it for adoption through a contact he had in Chicago. Myra, nor her mother, would hear of this. It was their baby, their life, and they wanted it. But even they knew when the day came, the evidence would show. The father of this baby was white, and another scandal would again be let go and up for discussion on the streets of Greensboro. For Myra, her Mother and the Doctor, it was an ulcer in the making! Myra hurt because the one she loved could not be near her during this time. He could only see her from afar, never able to touch her.

On a cold morning in November, Myra's Mother made her way to the back door of the Doctor's clinic. Knocking at the door, excited and scared, she beckoned the doctor to come to her house to see Myra. As the baby grew, the doctor learned Myra was too small to deliver, which meant hospitalization and the surgical removal of the child at birth. This meant money, a hospital stay, and the possible jeopardizing of the lives of both Myra and her baby.

Tommy Fowler made his way down Main Street. His friends began joking with him, kicking cans, and making daring bets of who would and would not do what. As he turned into the back alley to visit Myra's Father's café, he ordered a Coca-Cola and a hamburger. As he and his friends sat at the table, he overheard a discussion at another table between three colored ladies about Myra and her unfortunate sickness. This startled him because up until now, he had heard nothing. Tommy could not finish his hamburger and coca-cola. In haste he left to make his way to Myra's house. As he neared Myra's house, he saw the doctor coming from the front porch. He asked the Doctor was everything all right, and when asked why he wanted to know, Tommy just told him that Myra was a friend of his. The Doctor told Tommy it was not any of his affairs to be asking such questions and he would be best served to let well enough alone. As Tommy walked away, Myra, having heard him talking to the Doctor, drew back the curtain and peeked out.

A white boy in a Mississippi town never goes calling to the hill. This was a fact Tommy had always been taught, but, he knew he could not just abandon her. Myra was his friend and he liked her. He refused to turn his back on her. In the late evening Tommy again made his way back to the hill, and this time he saw Myra sitting on the porch, looking rather plump and heavy, in loose fitting clothing. Tommy walked up to the gate looked at her, asking if she was alright. Myra, with her head down, replied, "Yes". Tommy asked her what was wrong, and walked through the gate, up the steps and onto the porch with her. As he approached Myra, she stood up, and he became sick to his stomach, for now he knew her situation. There was no doubt in his mind. And as she looked at him, she swore a solemn oath. She would never give his secret away. He felt lower than the lowest, and felt as if he had betrayed her; for even though he knew it was his, he also could never come to her rescue, never be able to help her, never stand up for her, and that she and this baby would have to bear the burden totally all alone.

Myra's father arrived home as Tommy stood there talking with Myra. He began to curse her, slap her, for being seen in public in such a shape, and especially in the presence of a white boy. Tommy, scared and shaking, tried to restrain her father, but he continued to hit her, and harder. He slapped her, hit her with balled fists, and bloodied her lip. Tommy, losing his temper, picked up a piece of stove wood and hit Myra's father with it, causing him to fall against the post of the front porch, hitting his head really hard. As Myra's Mother came out, Tommy explained he had to do it; that her father was going to seriously hurt or kill Myra. Myra's Mother told

Tommy to leave, so he did. As he looked at Myra, he reassured her things would be alright, and not to worry.

As the morning dew settled on the grass and trees in Greensboro, all that could be heard on the streets was the sound of horse hooves, pulling the garbage wagon owned by Mr. George Brown. Slowly progressing down the street, picking up the garbage the store owners had discarded the night prior. One could hear the wooden peg leg of Mr. Brown as he "clomped" from pile to pile, every now and then hollering, "Whoa, Mules:" As Tommy sat helpless in the shadows of backstreets, he contemplated what he could do, if anything, to help Myra. He liked her but marriage was out of the question, and he felt sick inside for having put her into a situation of having to endure such a hardship as this. What could he do? Better yet, how could he do anything, besides cause her trouble? But in his heart, he had to do something. He would think, he would plan, and he would act.

The morning air was heavy, laden with fog and a slight mist of rain. Tommy walked at a fast pace, performing his morning chores. First, the garbage, then the wood for the wash pots, so Hilda, the maid, could heat water to do the laundry. After nearly two hours of sweat and toil, the chores were complete, and this meant Tommy was free to explore the daily haunts of Greensboro and the back alley café. As he walked down the back alley, passing the calaboose, a voice rang loudly calling Tommy's name. "Massa Tommy", "Massa Tommy comes here," a voice dazed from a night of hard drinking. "Yes", replied Tommy, "whose there?" "It's me. Massa Tommy, its Joe Ben." Laughing, Tommy said, "uh-Oh! Another night of carousing, done have you locked up!" "Yes suh", said Joe Ben. The morning dawned, the clouds lay low over the small town, and again people made their way to and from in haste gathering the treasures they had purchased. As morning gave way to noon, three men came running into town from the depot. Each could barely talk, from fright, and the horrid remembrance that had all of a sudden become etched in their minds. An older black man began to speak saying, "they kilt him, they kilt him, and Lord have mercy, they gone and kilt him". The crowd began to grow, and the reality of a not so peaceful existence showed its shadow over the small community.

∼ ∼ ∼

The hearse made its way along the quiet peaceful lane through Greensboro Cemetery. Reverend Kilgore preceded the procession in his faded light green Studebaker, while the pallbearers followed closely behind. Red faces with smeared mascara could be seen on the faces of those who passed by. Death at a ripe old age of eighty was reality rather than surprise, but to family, such goodbyes are difficult, no matter what. Arlen Gray was a war hero. He had served in the Army in World War II, had fought in the Battle of the Bulge, had survived the D-Day invasion at Normandy, and had been highly decorated, having been awarded the Distinguished Service Medal, the Bronze Star, the Purple heart, for shrapnel received during the Battle of the Bulge, not to mention other citations and service ribbons. He was a community pillar, having served as County Supervisor. Arlen's nephew, Sheriff Abernathy has served the county as Sheriff for three terms, and like his uncle had achieved community notoriety. Arlen's sister, Sheriff Abernathy's mother, was now the remaining and sole surviving sibling of the Gray family, and she in her mid seventies as do most others of her tenure, had begun to experience the common medical ailments prevalently noticed and reported to medical care givers. Sheriff Gray's mother, Anna Belle, a stout stature lady, acted in a manner of one accustomed to southern privilege, as was exemplified by her son and grandsons. She was escorted to and from whatever it was she needed to do, she received guests with the guidance of a maid who regularly attended her needs, cleaned her home, washed her clothes, ironed her clothes, and cooked her meals, in a dated nineteen fifties kitchen. Miss Anna Belle was a southern lady, projecting the image of prosperity and affluence.

When the family had been seated, the casket checked and placed correctly by the funeral director, the pallbearers assembled by rank and file just out from under the burial tent, Reverend Kilgore solemnly, with his finger marking his selected passage, placed both hands in front folding them, and asked those present to bow in prayer. The wind blew; the already turned and crisp leaves of the oaks, pin oaks, hickory flew through the air, rustling as they passed. The chill of winter pierced the coats, scarves, and shawls of everyone, causing several "brrrrr's" to be heard as the Reverend recounted the blessing of all the accomplishments of Arlen Gray, and what he had meant to this little, secluded community and township of Greensboro.

During the procession and service, Anna Belle's grandson, the Sheriff's son, Bubba, was tasked with seeing that his grandmother and mother were transported to the funeral and gravesite. The Sheriff, in his capacity, and as the deceased's nephew, served as pallbearer. Bubba, being a child of slow ability, and one, who had not and never would advance in mental capacity beyond that of a twelve year old, had at his present age of twenty two been given the servitude task of runner for the Sheriffs office. In this official capacity and since the Sheriff was Bubba's father, Bubba had been afforded the distinct privilege of wearing the uniform of an unarmed deputy? Everyone in Greensboro knew this was a token job; that is except Bubba. He carried a book of tickets, to write when offenders needed chastising, but the tickets never went beyond the wastebasket in the Sheriff's office. Bubba was more of a nuisance than anything else, but everyone knew him, knew what he was like, and smiled when he would write a ticket, say thank you, and go about his way. From time to time would- be offenders became verbal with him, and he would haul them in, but once inside the Sheriffs office, someone else usually took over and things were dropped, and apologized for. Bubba was a kind hearted person, never realizing his efforts was not taken seriously. Truthfully, the extent of his serious endeavors amounted to sweeping the office, taking out the garbage, bringing food to the prisoners, when they were present and running errands. When Grandma Anna Belle called, this was Bubba's priority one, he was Granny's boy!

The ground around the gravesite was bulky, mostly because as the grave was dug, loose dirt would undoubtedly roll here and there, so that when the funeral director laid down the artificial turf flooring on which to place the chairs for the family to sit, clumps or mounds of unbroken dirt could be noticed everywhere. Some, as they sat, would teeter in their chairs, especially the elderly, so when it happened, you would see people surge, weaving in and out of rows trying to catch them before they fell out and down onto the green and worn artificial turf. Bubba took no chances. He personally seated his mother and grandmother, and stood beside them at attention during the proceedings. He took no chances with his two precious charges. Reverend Kilgore, being a good Baptist preacher, chose a sermon of enlightenment and recollection. From time to time, while reading Arlen's biography, snickers could be heard; family would laugh, then cry, then laugh, and then cry again. When in truth, and in our hearts, good Baptist preacher can, if afforded the opportunity, prepare a sendoff befitting royalty. Such was the experience of Arlen Gray. As Brother Kilgore neared the mid-point of his sermon at the graveside, in the distance four loud distinct gunshots could be heard. After all it was hunting season in Mississippi, and avid sportsmen took to the woods in search of a catch and trophy unlike any other. Deer season was a time of male domination, and most conversation in all of the little service stations amounted to nothing more than who had seen but missed the undisputable twelve or even sixteen-point buck, that was just within the sights of he who just never could get the perfect shot.

As four shots rang out, Brother Kilgore, who was right in the middle of quoting a passage, clapped the palm of his hand hard against his bible. Compounded with the loud ring of gunshots, the thump of his hand on the Bible, and silence on the hill at the gravesite, it sounded like three cannons at Shiloh had volleyed in unison, and Grandma passed out cold as a cucumber! As she fainted, she crumpled over onto Bubba's leg, which caused him to go berserk. After a time, it dawned on Bubba that Grandma was not in a state of awareness, so he grabbed her shoulders as he sat down with her falling over into his lap. Loudly, and in a still of silence rarely heard, Bubba screamed, "Sniper! Hot damn, they've shot Grandma!" Like rabbits in a corn field, people scattered. They ran through the cemetery, some running into and over tombstones, some even falling and rolling in the leaves. The pallbearers scattered to the four winds, as did the Reverend, and most of the family. It was a frenzied site to behold. Looking across the cemetery, one could see people running in such a panic, they had forgotten their cars, which were parked in the parking lot of the cemetery. Bubba, managing to get grandma and his mother into the squad car sped to the hospital as if in a state of emergency. Once grandma was examined and released by the doctor in the local hospital emergency room, she was released and permitted to be taken home by Bubba.

Bubba's last day on the force, for at least a few months, came the next week. His father, having received pressure from the board of supervisors, thought it was a move that needed to be made. Bubba remained in his room from embarrassment for a while, but after coaxing and bragging from his grandmother and mother, he again regained the confidence needed to face the world, and emerged, but not with unsolicited snickers from passersby who just could not restrain themselves from that eventful afternoon atop Greensboro Cemetery hill.

~ ~ ~

Days lapsed, but not without rumor and gossip as to who had committed the despicable act of murdering the colored man who had been found laying along the railroad tracks near the train depot. No identification had been made, and it almost appeared there wouldn't be any due to the condition of the body. What clothes and items found at the scene were in police custody, but no pending arrests were imminent. What had been found had been saved for evidence, and would be sent to the capitol for testing. People were remarking about the unsafe conditions in Greensboro, saying they felt it was unsafe for children to play unattended and women to walk alone and be left alone. Everyone became up-at-arms about the entire situation. Some felt the sheriff and police departments were not providing the level of security they had been charged with, and the town residents were growing very concerned. There were too many places on the dimly lit streets, the low overhanging foliage, and the overgrowth of grass, along streets, alleyways and railroad tracks. Something had to be done, and it had to be done fast.

To promote a feeling of security the sheriff temporarily hired extra deputies to patrol the streets during the night time hours, but even by doing this, he could not ensure total security. The uncertainty and fear which rested with all was knowing there was killer on the loose, but where was he and who was he. For an act of hate to be committed such as this, a person would surely have to be mentally deranged.

Many of the townspeople felt this was an act of the Klu Klux Klan. The Klan was a violent organization who held no secret of its consideration of the colored populous. They had openly voiced their opinions time and time again, and periodically would distribute literature and handouts throughout town. Sometimes, after Klan meetings, they would litter the streets, especially in the colored residential areas, with hate literature. It was a fearful time; no one knew who to trust and who not to trust. The colored people organized watch groups to patrol the residential streets. In case any activity occurred they would sound an alarm and the police would come having the help of the people.

~ ~ ~

As school busses arrived, they disembarked their charges disembarked for yet another day of activities. Children were welcomed with small white papers strewn throughout the schoolyard. Many stopped to pick them up, placed them in their satchels, and then walked on to classes. During study hall, you could hear talking in a low tone, with the reading of each sentence. Eyes became large, many questioned the content and its meaning: "The White Knights of the Klu Klux Klan of the State of Mississippi". It went on to avow the unity of all white people, stating their beliefs, and what they perceived the Bible to ensure. By class' end, most of the papers were discarded in the garbage can, and removed from the library study hall. No arrests, no suspects, and no justice in sight. Surely right would prevail. No one deserved to die in such a manner, even coloreds; and especially coloreds who were known and liked.

Tommy continued to ponder his avenues of dismissal of what had occurred between he and Myra. The months passed, and although he had tried to see her, she continued to be elusive. Over and over in his mind he tried beyond reason to justify what had happened, always arriving at the same conclusion. He had brought wrath unknowing on a young girl, with whom he had nothing in common, and yet now, their very lives were woven together and would be forever, whether they liked it or not.

By now, everyone was aware of their secret. Tommy had no route of escape, and his parents were surely not about to just sit by and let their son endure this fiasco of moral and mental defeat. The decision was made to send Tommy to his uncle's in Baton Rouge. He could finish school there, then return and attend college. Tommy, with little to say or do, succumbed to the plan. So, with his mothers help, he packed his belongings, rode with his parents to the train depot, said his goodbyes, boarded the Memphis and Jackson Railway, and rode off into the afternoon sunset toward the river, then to Arkansas, where he would change and go south to Baton Rouge. In his mind he kept going over everything. Maybe this was the answer: out of sight, out of mind. At least, for the time being, it gave a sense of ease and calm. What about Myra? She was left to bear the brunt of embarrassment, public ridicule and scorn. This too, would be the fate of his child. Though born to a colored girl, the baby was still his, and a part of him. Even at his young age, being abused, ridiculed, laughed at, and scorned by being half-white and half-colored, was almost more than he dare to consider. In his mind he searched for ways to avoid this, but what could he do? He was still just a boy, still in school, and still a white in a town of segregation. Her welfare had not escaped his thought. Laboriously he spent his time in thought of what could be done for Myra. Realizing the two could never unite beyond what had already occurred; Tommy lay awake in thought trying his best to ponder all alternatives.

The newspaper continued to print weekly stories of the murder. People still gathered continuing to offer scenarios as to how it could have happened, but whatever they offered, it all amounted to nothing more than speculation. The sheriff continued to investigate while the deputies painstakingly attempted to uncover any and all unturned stones relating to the case. Frustration abounded and tempers grew short. Most everyone, especially those within the colored community thought the sheriff and police departments had begun to drag their feet. It had become embarrassing. They were being made a mockery, and in their thoughts they were giving their all. You just couldn't crack a case if you did not have the basics. There was no murder weapon, and no eye witness. No one would admit to any noises, or having seen anyone during that time with the person who had been killed.

The majority thought another colored had committed the crime. The coloreds thought the Klu Klux Klan was the responsible entity, and the sheriff and police departments were nothing more than referees. It was getting old, and if something didn't happen soon, there just might be trouble to contend with, and they sure didn't need that. Not in a time when civil rights was beginning to get a strong foothold. If this got out, it meant newspaper reporters, the colored organization and an all out bad time. Greensboro had to do something and soon.

The town fathers gathered in the office of the mayor to discuss what options they had to consider. It was a serious situation, one that dictated immediate consideration. Not having made significant progress lessened their chances for continuing public support. The town needed closure, but more than that, they needed to guilty party behind bars. People were felt betrayed by the willingness of the sheriff's department and police department to actively pursue and incarcerate the criminal. This was a problem of grave concern, and the constituencies' patience was growing thin. If they didn't solve this matter soon there would be voter vengeance, which could cost them their positions. Small towns have a way of rendering credit where credit is due. Greensboro was not indifferent.

～ ～ ～

January in Greensboro was bitter cold. The smell of wood burning in fireplaces permeated the air, while little activity noticed outside. It was the dead of winter and few were brave enough to go outside for periods of extended time. School saw a vast decline of student attendance due to flu, colds and ailments associated with the colder seasons. Life was on hold in Greensboro, so most remained inside, sat by the fire, did household chores, and read the weekly paper as their source of news relating to the outside world. A radio was a rare commodity, and for those who were wealthy enough to afford one, and the batteries required to operate it, usually its usage was solely restricted to Friday, Saturday and Sunday nights. Most radios were only able to receive one station, that being the AM station WBPC, located sixty-five miles North in the town of Salter. Most families would make an evening of listening to the radio, canning, baking, preparing meals for the next day, and family time, which in this time was not a rarity. Once the livestock were fed, and penned up for the night, the cows milked, life revolved mostly around the kitchen. The kitchen was the focal point of country life, mainly because it was the warmest room in the house, and roomy enough for the family to sit at the table, and read, listen to the radio, talk about community items of interest, and spend time.

The winter seemed to bring people together strengthening family unity. It was not uncommon when walking past a home and see people sitting around a fire place talking with children playing in the floor. Time to share thoughts and spend quality time with the ones you love. The winter also bonded relationships with fathers and sons while on hunting trips. Although Tommy's father wasn't much of a sportsman, he still cared about being with his son. Tommy in many ways shared his father's beliefs when it came to hunting. "Why kill something so beautiful, when you can stand quietly and watch the magnificence of Gods creation in its own environment?" Most men in the south were hunters. Few ever stand in the wild, especially during hunting season, just to watch beautiful animals. You could get killed!

Tommy preferred walks in the woods, just taking in the scenic beauty which he loved so dear. The fresh smell of cedar, the smoke from fireplaces as it quietly crept through the trees settling gently on the breeze with an aroma of the impending holiday season as it neared. There was more to nature than killing it. Rather, it was if he chose to be one with nature. Here in the woods, he was at peace, with himself and with God. He felt as if the very creatures knew of his presence and welcomed him into their habitat. They didn't seem to mind, they tolerated him. It was if they knew he only wanted to share their kingdom, not destroy it. His heart became lifted with each step, walking along old trails with fallen trees, leaping across ditches filled with almost frozen water. He was captivated by how life seemed to continue on, even here in this outdoor garden of cold frozen wilderness.

~ ~ ~

When and if snow ever came to Greensboro, its presence bedecked the rooftops as that of a winter wonderland. Greensboro was located on several small, but not so high, hills. Its streets were paved but not as well kept as more traveled city streets. This made way for sled paths, which would inevitably make way for the sprains and broken bones that enhanced the patient load of the town's lone doctor. Dr. Jim was both friend and physician. Much of his business included the birth of most of the town's citizens, and at his age he had for the most part played a large role in the birth, well being, and death of the town's citizens. He was more than the town doctor, he was a friend. Dr. Jim made house calls, regardless of the hour, usually charging minimal fees, and when patients or parents could not pay, a lot of the time his fee was usually a chicken, fresh meat, vegetables in the summer, and repairs, if needed on his residence or clinic.

Dr. Jim's clinic at one time in earlier years was a home. He had returned from the war, opened practice in the little town, and settled into a life of meager existence. Dr. Jim loved Greensboro. It was his birthplace, so he felt a calling to remain here and follow in the footsteps of his father who had been the town's first doctor. The clinic was both office and patient care center. Beds were set up in make-shift rooms to care for the sick. The clinic staff was small, but personable. They all lived in Greensboro, so working here was like taking care of family. Regardless of ability to pay, no one was ever refused treatment, and minor surgical procedures were performed with love and care. Dr. Jim's ability was revered and what he said was gospel.

His days were unending. Always with a smile and desire to heal he traveled the roads and byways in search of patient residences. Must as his father had done in previous years, except with Doctor Jim, he had a car, unlike his father in his horse and buggy. Regardless of weather, time or need, he never failed to live up to the trust that had been bestowed upon him. His medical credo was his life; he lived it to the fullest. His ability to relate made him popular.

On a pleasant fall day a young boy who had been playing chase while his grandfather slept under a tree accidentally slipped and fell onto a broken coca-cola bottle cutting his wrist badly. Alarmed, the grandfather, who was supposed to have been watching the young boy, picked him up in his arms and took him inside to where the child's grandmother was. Walking up the steps the old man called, "Mama, Mike's feel and hurt his hand." Answering him back, over all the crying and carrying on, she replied, "Well, sit him down here and let's fix it up, and get him to the doctor." Fixing up to her was slicing an Irish potation two, putting some concoction of vinegar and whatever else on it, then tying it up and around his wrist with a white cloth that she had torn in half. Arriving at Doctor Jim's office, bypassing the receptionist, they took him directly on and into the doctor's office. Sitting at his desk, Doctor Jim asked, "What's the emergency?" The grandmother said, "Mike's fallen, cut his arm almost in half, can you please sew it up for him?" Unwrapping the homemade bandage, smelling the powerful aroma of vinegar and all else that was apart of the poultice, Doctor Jim asked, "Good Lord, what the hell is this?" The grandmother advised that it was a poultice, one of her making and that it was good home medicine. Shaking his head, reaching for instruments to examine the wound with, the doctor laughed and said, "Mike, you're a strong little boy. There's enough vinegar on here to last a normal household a month."

His advice always reassured those who came to him. He never promised eternity, but he did give hope.

~ ~ ~

As winter came to a close, fields were plowed, and made ready for the next planting season. Few men could be found outside the field. Life in Greensboro revolved around farming. Women usually did not work, other than in the home. Providing was the man's responsibility. Children were seen playing openly in yards, and life seemed to once again enjoy a rebirth, as the trees budded, flowers sprang forth from the ground, grass grew, dogs laid lazily on front porches or in yards. Life was good.

Tilling the soil lasted for months. Painstaking effort to properly prepare the fields for planting meant little time at home for the men and boys who were old enough to help with the work. Mules were teamed and sharecroppers were assigned their sections of land. Cotton was big business in Mississippi. Crops were planted with a great deal of effort and time to ensure good results. Weather conditions were a primary source for a successful crop. Constant care was required, often requiring those who worked the land to plow sometimes well into the night. Life was a challenge, but for those who benefited from the rewards it proved to be a worthwhile investment.

Corn was also a beneficial crop. Corn served many purposes. When planted it required occasional plowing, good fertilization, and complimentary weather conditions. Corn, when harvested, would be ground into cornmeal, or saved for feel for livestock. It provided rapid weight gain and the farmer benefited from its use when cattle and pigs were sent to market for sale.

During the nineteen sixties aerial defoliation became popular in the Mississippi region. Farmers learned that by spraying their crops aerially, it took less time and was more cost effective. Crop dusters could load, take off, be at a location, spray the crop and return in minimal time. Prior to aerial use, farmers defoliated their crops using mules to pull the machinery through the field, down the rows, close to the cotton, sometimes causing damage.

Greensboro was a hub for the aerial crop spraying industry. Several men, all local, decided to enter into a venture and begin a crop spraying business. Among those who invested was a local gentleman named Junior Barnum. Junior had been a private pilot for some years and thought this was his calling. Already owning an airplane, he had it outfitted with all the necessary mechanical apparatus's, and within a month or two he had started a business and was advertising his services. Junior was thinking big! This would make him a millionaire.

On a hazy Thursday afternoon, from an old cow pasture, Junior took to the air, for the maiden flight of his bright red bi-plane. There he sat, in the cockpit, goggles on his face, his mustache very noticeable, a big grin, and an old World War II aviators cap on his head. He looked like the Red Baron taking off for yet another dog fight. What most people didn't know was that just inside his coat, in the right pocket, for good luck he carried a small bottle of Old Crow, to christen this, the maiden voyage. Being excited and dwelling on how well his business would do, Junior had partaken of the "spirits" just a tad too much. By the time he had taken off he was well on his way to a happier flight.

Crops were sprayed, the airplane performing gracefully under the guidance of Junior's steadfast hands and feet. He waved to the farmers from aloft, really making them notice his ability to do the job quickly and efficiently. It was good advertising. Completing the job, he looped the field, waved vigorously to those below, the made a half turn and directed his airplane toward Greensboro and to the make-shift hangar that he had built. Upon landing, he noticed several trucks parked beside the hangar and along side the airstrip. As he taxied to a stop, he was met with several disgruntled farmers, who advised him that he had sprayed everyone's crop in the area with exception of the very ones he was hired to spray. Junior discussed the issue, and a settlement was reached. He continued to fly.

On yet another occasion, one of Junior's friends had entered into a business partnership with him, and another airplane was purchased. This airplane was slightly larger, a single engine aircraft, but one that could carry two passengers. His business partner would, from time to time, fly with him, taking joy rides through the local Greensboro countryside. Junior's partner, on one occasion, approached him, asking if he would fly him to the capitol city to visit a relative that had been hospitalized. Always ready to fly and lend a helping hand, Junior and his partner set a time, and shook hands. They met at the airstrip that afternoon early, to allow for daytime flying to and from the capitol city. Both inside the airplane and buckled in, Junior cranked the engine, checked his instruments, and taxied away from the hangar and to the end of the pasture. As they sat there, Junior's business partner laughed and joked, and with everything in check and running good, Junior pushed the throttle forward and away they flew. About twenty minutes into the flight, and flying over a major state highway, Junior turned to his partner and said, "Sam, do you know how to pray?" With a questioning look, and not really sure if he had heard him correct, Sam replied, "What did you say?" Junior responded again, "Do you know how to pray?" "Of course, I'm a Baptist." With no change in expression Junior turned from the controls and said to Sam, "Well, in that case, get on with it because we're out of gas, and there's nowhere to land except the highway!" Terror showed itself all over Sam's face. As Junior tilted the nose of the airplane toward the ground, he very delicately nursed his crippled airplane, with engine sputtering, and his passenger having heart spasms, down and softly onto the state highway. Not even a bump, not even a close call, and Junior was laughing! Sam, on the other hand, was inconsolable, he wanted to go home. Junior taxied the plane to the side of the road leaving instructions for Sam to remain with the plane until he got back with gasoline. Junior caught a ride and within a short time returned. Upon his return, he found Sam doing his best to explain to a state trooper exactly what had happened. When Junior walked up, the trooper, directing his attention to Junior, said, "What do you propose to do?" Junior replied, "I propose we fill this airplane up with gas and get the hell ought of here!" "Where and how do you plan to do that?" replied the trooper. "I plan to pour this gas into this tank. I plan to get my passenger inside, and we both will buckle up. I then plan to crank this engine and taxi down this highway and leave," replied Junior. "No sir", replied the trooper, "not on my highway!" "Then why don't you get back into your car, drive down to the break of the curve, turn crossways in the road to stop traffic, and watch me?" replied Junior. Sam, by this time had made a decision not to fly back with Junior, so he began to undo his seatbelt and get out. Seeing that Sam could not be convinced to get back in with him, Junior, asked him to go to the other end of the road and stop traffic. Sam walked off, and seeing he really couldn't stop him, the trooper drove off to the other end toward the curve, and waited to watch Junior kill himself.

The airplane cranked, and Junior began moving. He waved to Sam as he passed, and then turned and began to rev the engine up for take-off. The take-off was unremarkable, but according to Sam the car load of people that topped the hill just in time to see Junior take off and go right over the top of their car, well, it was a sight to see. Rumor has it they picked car parts out of pine trees there for quite some time.

Junior Barnum lived to the ripe old age of eighty two. Throughout his years of flying he was never injured, nor were any of his passengers. He is remembered as an aviation pioneer in the town of Greensboro, and a very colorful character. His unique abilities as a pilot made him a well respected man in Greensboro. Junior, loved to fly. He lived for the rush of energy only flying could provide. He was the topic of many conversations, due to his landing through the years in corn fields, pig pens, gravel roads, highways, and yes even the trees. Somehow, he was spared, and so goes the saying, "God is my co-pilot!" In Junior's case, "God was the pilot!"

With fond memories I recall when as a child, I would hear the hum of that old airplane making its way to our fields. I knew Junior was on his way. I would run as fast as I could to the fence, climb upon it, and perch there just to get as close to him as I could and watch him fly by. He never failed to wave, and he never failed to dip his wing in a final "good-bye" when he finished the job. He was my hero, and he was my mother's cousin.

The skies over Greensboro are a little quieter now with his absence, but he's still up there, if you listen quietly. The skies are filled will pilots that he trained and released.

~ ~ ~

Myra's baby, a boy, was born in early summer. It didn't make headlines, not even the birth column in the local newspaper. She continued to work at the café, and raise her son in the home where she grew up. No one, with exception of those whom she saw daily, knew of her new child. By now, the gossip had subsided. Tommy was in Louisiana with his uncle and family and life moved on. Still, no breaking news as to who had committed the murder. Townspeople still came to town on Saturday to do their weekly shopping, cattle sales still were held at the stockyards weekly, and Dr. Jim continued to mend broken bones, sew stitches, pronounce deaths, and bring babies into the world. Life was a never ending cycle in Greensboro.

With the birth of Myra's little boy her life changed for the better. Yes, it was added responsibility, she was very young but she had her mother to help her. She knew that no matter what, her mother would always be there, even now with all of this. It wasn't easy being a mother at her age, she was just a girl, and her baby was half white, which caused added concern. Hopefully, she prayed, through time this will all ease from the memory of those who know. She knew that Doctor Jim would always be there for her needs, as he had always been.

~ ~ ~

Miss Jean, a propertied lady of the local Methodist congregation regularly drove the streets of Greensboro in search of flowers to create weekly altar arrangements. She was a lady of impeccable class and dignity who often would stop as she drove along and offer gardening hints to those who stopped to listen. Although she had no children of her own, every child in town felt kindred to her. She never went without words of encouragement and support. No matter what a yard displayed, Miss Jean always could offer just the right hint of suggestion, and in ways one might consider the idea their own, until they had time enough to stop and reflect on the conversation.

It was on one such afternoon, a neighbor, being on knees with bent back under close supervision of his wife Miss Jean, drove by and decided to visit for a while. Being one to never gossip, when told of things that were happening or had happened, her famous reflection was always one of "I'll Suwannee." When you heard this, you knew she was hearing something she had not been aware of before. She never visited without bringing a helping serving of delicious chicken salad. The townspeople of Greensboro almost prayed for an alms visit from Miss Jean, because it always meant chicken salad. Miss Jean's family lived in another part of the state. She had come to Greensboro in her youth after having married into a local family. She was educated, very talented, and considered to be a lady of distinction, and considered by all of those who embraced and held her near and dear as a mother figure.

Miss Jean's family had been one of affluence. Although the death of her father before her birth did not go without leaving a prominent male figure in her life, her grandfather, a southern gentleman and businessman had taken Miss Jean, her sister, and her mother, (his daughter), into his home, and it was here they lived until Miss Jean graduated school and went on to college. During her college days at a local university Miss Jean met a tall stoutly young man who had been born and raised in Greensboro. His name was Conrad. Conrad, a timid, country boy, himself was also a student in college, and through letters, and an introduction at a basketball game, He and Miss Jean met, became friends, sweethearts, fell in love and married. Thirty years had passed since Miss Jean had located residency in Greensboro. She had turned a small country home into a showplace of horticultural fantasy. It seemed everything she touched grew and blossomed, to include the souls on which she left an impression.

~ ~ ~

On her way home one afternoon, Miss Jean drove past a young colored girl walking along a dusty back street, carrying a baby in her arms. Not bearing to see the baby exposed to the rain, Miss Jean stopped, and said, "Girl, get in, let me take you where you are going!" Myra, knowing Miss Jean, said "Thank you, Miss Jean", opened the door, and got inside. As Miss Jean drove, Myra pulled back the blanket from her sons face, and spoke to him. Miss Jean smiled, laughed, and spoke to the baby, as she always did. Having no children of her own, she omitted few opportunities to pay attention to children. Miss Jean asked Myra, "What's his name?" Hesitantly, Myra said, "Hadn't named him yet, can't make up my mind, Mam." Miss Jean said, "Honey, the baby needs a name. Better name him before he get old enough to name himself," and smiled. Myra smiled back. Miss Jean, as she looked at the baby, could see that this child was white. Although she never asked, and she never discussed it, it bothered her because she knew the fate this child would experience. As Miss Jean pulled up to where Myra was going, they got out, and Myra thanked her for the ride. Miss Jean, said goodbye first to the baby, then to Myra.

Driving on home, Miss Jean thought hard about the situation. The world as it was wasn't fair, and for Myra, with this child, and at her age, life would not be the bed of roses that most young women hoped for. She felt sorry for her, she wasn't a bad girl, she had made a mistake, it could have happened to anyone. She was black, but she was still human and one of God's children. She thought silently of how she wished she could ease her burden, but as it was there was little she could do. Myra's battle for forgiveness with family and friends would be a long struggle. At the most, Miss Jean realized all she could do would be to encourage her at every opportunity.

She even considered offering a job cleaning her house to Myra, but with the child, it was premature. Myra had employment, meager as it was, but for now it would do. She was with her parents, and they would help her and the baby. They wouldn't be put out on the street to fend for themselves.

∼ ∼ ∼

The office of Miss Jean's attorney was musky smelling. She would stop in daily to sign business and discuss transactions. Miss Jean, her husband, and the attorney, Wade Goss, had been personal and business friends for some thirty-plus years. She more than her husband, operated the daily affairs of their business. As she would always put it, "He's more interested in a pasture than in this office." She would laugh and say, "Just let me mention mowing the grass, and he always found some reason to go to a pasture."

In confidence Miss Jean spoke candidly to Wade asking him his opinion of matters of a personal nature to her. She was a private person, yet one with a heart of love and giving. Wade, hearing her proposal, offered several alternatives, advised her to consider them, then either call him or stop by and see him again and he would do as she instructed. Smiling, Miss Jean said, "I'll think it over, and I'll see you in the next few days." Leaving the office, she backed out of the parking place, and drove back to her office.

Once back at her office, she thought for a short time, picked up the phone, dialed Wade Goss, and when he answered said, "Wade, this is Jean. Just go ahead and draw up what we talked about, no need to think any harder about it, I'll just do it." Responding to her request, Wade said, "Okay, no problem, it'll be ready, if you like this afternoon. What are we going to tell Conrad?" Laughing, Miss Jean replied, "We're going to tell him the cows are out, from that point on what we do or say will have no influence on him."

When Myra's son was in grade school, on the "hill", he, a lot of times, would come home crying, saying, "Mama, they call me names, they say I ain't colored. "What am I, mama?" Myra would always smile and say, "Honey, you're you, you are special, and you are what you are." Of course, her answers, never fully satisfied his curiosity, but for the time, it provided an answer and he lost track of the conversation, and she was spared an in-depth explanation. She dreaded the day when she would have to sit down and tell, in honesty, exactly what made him as he was. Often, she, as she would think about it, would cry, because in her heart she knew her son would live his life with the presence, and knowing, that he was unlike most others in Greensboro. Myra, felt ashamed for her son, not of the cause or reason for him, but for the embarrassment that overshadowed him, and she knew his life would not be easy, especially in this town.

As he lay in his bed, Myra walked quietly into his room, standing for a while looking at hers and Tommy's son, and with tears in her eyes, she prayed for forgiveness for causing so much grief that would become part of this little boy's life. He had no idea the path that lay ahead, nor did she. Myra kissed his forehead and cheek, and with the whisper of her breath, spoke, "Sleep peaceful my little Thomas, under the guardianship of God's angels." She turned and walked from the room, to her room.

Walking from his room, Myra couldn't help but pray for his understanding. He was an innocent little boy born into a life that would never be pleasant for him. Time after time she had blamed herself, not for having him but for bringing him into a world that was not receptive to her kind or his. Myra, thinking quietly as she lay down became burdened. No thought could erase the difficulty she knew Thomas would endure. Her feelings for Tommy were real, she knew it, but for what it would mean for Thomas was almost unbearable. She doubted herself many times as a mother. She even wished over and over that she had been born white. Birth was the work of God, she had nothing to do with it, only accept it, and live as he intended.

~ ~ ~

The train would be in any minute. It was summer, and Tommy could barely remain in one spot, overcome with anticipation of seeing his parents, old friends, and the not so crowded streets of his beloved Greensboro. A hint of rain presented itself, but nothing could spoil this day. He was home, and if he had his way, he was staying! The trained puffed its way around curves, filled with pine trees, oaks, pecan trees and patches of wildflowers. Each slow surge of steam carried him closer and closer to the railway depot where he would emerge, almost a man. Surely his parents would see his manly presence. He had grown up, and had become a clean cut young gentleman. He wondered who would accompany his parents to meet him.

As the engine slowed to a stop, the conductor leapt from the car, readying the footstool for all to disembark. Everyone waited, and to their surprise, there he stood in the doorway, hair, cut, combed with oil, all slicked back, a new suit of clothes, with bag in hand. His mother, unable to remain still, ran forward, embracing him as if he were a son returning from war. His father extended his hand and shook it firmly. Other friends surrounded him, patting him on the back, wishing him well, telling him what all he had missed, and of the new haunts to explore. But first it was home, to mama's table and a fresh cooked meal of string beans, fresh sliced onion, fresh tomatoes from the garden, purple hull peas, skillet cooked fresh field corn, roast beef from one of his fathers steers, and all the sweet tea he could hold, topped off with his mothers famous pecan pie. This was it; He was in heaven! After the meal, everyone gathered in the parlor, to sit and talk, to hear Tommy tell of life in Baton Rouge, and what he had done with his time, and about his studies. He was now ready to go to college, and that meant more hard work, and little time for play. His father had dabbled in conversation, trying to feel him out as to what he had planned to do with his life, but Tommy was not ready to discuss this. He had other plans, and conversation wasn't a part of the agenda.

When Tommy had arrived at the depot he thought he had caught a glimpse of a pretty, young, light-skinned black girl standing far in the background. He wasn't sure but he though it was Myra. He dared not even bring up the subject in the presence of his mother and father, for this would mean nothing but unwanted talk, and at this particular time he just couldn't handle it. Instead, he wanted to walk his familiar streets, to just look again at the old houses, see if he could spot and recognize the people who might be sitting on their front porches, and say hello, hoping they just might recognize him and ask how he was and what he had been doing. He felt like a celebrity returning. It was wonderful! Later in the afternoon, as the sun began to set, Tommy finally got up the nerve to walk to the back alley café where Myra worked, to order himself a delicious hamburger and coke. No place on earth cooked hamburgers like the café. You could smell them all over town, and it just drew you to the place. Myra's father was a cook, but considered among the colored and most of the white to be a chef. As Tommy, walked into the café, several recognized him, got up, shook his hand, seated him at a table, and brought him a coke as he had requested. Myra's father, from the cutout in the wall where food was passed through, recognized him sitting at the table, but did not approach him. Tommy had seen him too, but he didn't want to cause a scene. As the hamburger was brought to him, Tommy looked up, and there before him, dressed in her homemade dress, with white apron, was Myra. He couldn't speak; He just sat, smiled and looked at her. Myra's features were so beautiful, and Tommy was still captivated by her presence. She smiled, her mouth quivered, and she walked away. He meant to at least say hello, but didn't. Everyone in the café noticed the reaction of each as they faced each other.

As Tommy ate his hamburger, and drank the coke, again Myra returned asking if he wanted anything else. He replied, "No thank you", and as she started to walk off, he asked, "Myra, how are you?" Myra replied, "I'm all right, I guess, just the usual." Tommy replied, "I've thought about you, thought a lot." As he spoke he couldn't face her, he felt guilty, for what he has caused her to have to endure. As Myra stood there, he asked if she would sit down, but she couldn't because she was working. Tommy tried to make small talk, but each time he just mumbled words, and nothing he said came out right. He wiped his face, took one last drink, got up, left a fifty-cent tip, and walked out.

She walked home shortly after dusk, humming a tune as she went along her way. As she emerged from the alley street from the location of the café, she noticed a shadow that had appeared near some shrubs by the funeral home. She did not cross the street, she became scared. As she continued to walk home, she felt the presence of a person walking behind her. When Myra reached a point in the street, where neither could be noticed or heard, Tommy called softly to her. Myra, hearing his voice, stopped, and turned around. As Tommy approached her, holding his hands, his head looking to the ground, he then raised his head, and said, "Myra, please forgive me, I had no idea. Knowing what I now know, I promise you, I would never have allowed it to happen. I know you have had to endure more than you should, while I ran like a dog with his tail tucked between his legs. With your permission, if what I have heard is right, I would like to see my son." Myra, as she stood hearing this, and with tears in her eyes, stepped closer to Tommy, and said, "Tommy, Thomas will always be your son, nothing can change that, but we have to think about him and what his life will be like. He doesn't understand, and you can't expect him too." Tommy looked at Myra, and said, "Myra, I know I can't change things, but I want to know him, and someday I want him to know who he is." Myra, turned and ran home, she was not ready for this.

∼ ∼ ∼

The crops grew; for sure this year would be a bumper crop. Everyone was talking about how everything was just perfect. Tommy had had a full summer at home, he was a man now, and he was beginning to make his own way. His father, in his circle of friends, had bragged on how Tommy was going on to college, and going to make something of himself. Tommy felt successful. On the other street back, the alley, Myra, was going no where, she had a child to take care of, she was looked down on by her family, and she was at a dead end. There was a lot she wanted to say to Tommy, but somehow, considering the circumstances, and the two worlds in which they lived, whatever she said would be merely words, with insufficient meaning. She had her goals too, but they would never equal Tommy's.

As Thomas grew, Myra grew older, and Tommy went on to college and again returned home. Tommy was now a banker in the local bank, serving in an entry level position. He was being groomed for bigger and better things. The young ladies of the town had begun to notice him, and he was becoming a ladies' man. Through the years, the past resurfaced about Tommy's and Myra's illegitimate son. He never spoke of Thomas, or Myra, at least in the white sector.

~ ~ ~

Still, time gave way to no conclusive evidence as to what motivated the untimely death of the colored man found on the tracks, beneath the overhanging branches of the tall oaks in the curve of the railroad. Some say the police turned their back on a man who in their eyes served no purpose, but is this really the case? Did his color prove true to be the key factor for which no justice was ever served? Many believe the killer still walked the very streets as did they, causing everyone to glimpse, as they walked, wondering if this could be the killer? Who knows, no evidence was ever found. No weapon, no anything. Criminology of the day lacked in forensics, thus many cases grew cold quickly, and once grown cold, little or no hope of ever bringing the guilty to justice was ever realized. The case was still active; however, little effort was being put into its daily working. Loss of interest with more pressing issues surfaced such as board of supervisor suggestions, new businesses coming into town, the opening of a new planer mill, and the consolidation of the county school system. Justice was not on the forefront of the agenda.

~ ~ ~

The fire truck, alarms ringing loudly, rolled down main street enroute to a fire at the corner service station. It was rumored faulty electrical wiring caused the blaze. However, in an all volunteer fire department, many of whom were nothing more than local residents assisting in the containment, being unskilled and untrained at such things caused more harm than did well. The intent was good, just training lacked. Miss Jean sped quickly from her home. The call had come that their service station was ablaze. The effort now was to save the files and office if at all possible. She arrived, dressed in housecoat, hair in rollers, and lacking any sort of makeup. Conrad was already on the scene, instructing the removal of office equipment. Once she arrived, he quickly went to the fuel holding area and assisted in the work there. As the fire teemed higher and higher, like manna from heaven, clouds were noticed, heavy and low. The rain began to fall, and heavy. As quickly as it had started, it was over. The fuel tanks were heated, and well within range of explosion, however, for whatever reason, they never exploded. The building was a loss, but they could recover. Miss Jean, in her robe, hair in rollers, emerged with smut and charcoal all over her face and hands. Getting into her car she dusted her off her hands, never looked back, and said, "Heading to the house, tomorrow is another day."

Saturdays were always exciting and action packed. Rarely could places to park be found on Main Street. The theater always had a double feature, and at one-thirty in the afternoon a matinee was shown. Just about every kid in town could be found there, while their parents shopped and whiled away the hours in conversation, making up for lost time. The adults would usually stay late, and they themselves attend the feature movie at six-o'clock. You could always count on a good John Wayne movie, or Humphrey Bogart, or whatever had been released recently. The theater was located on the high side of the street. When as a child it seemed as large as an emporium, however in later years as I stand in front of where it once was, I came to realize just how small of a place it really was. I am amazed at how so many people could pack themselves into the seating. Makes one wonder if we really had the population they said we had.

The colored people attended the same theater as did we, only they entered through a side entrance, walking up a flight of stairs and into the projection booth area. The seating was poor, but would accommodate about fifty to seventy five people. White children who sat upstairs were frowned upon and reported to their parents. For many, the view was better, and never gave a second thought.

The popcorn could be smelled all over town. It was like a carnival. At least that's how it is remembered. You could purchase cokes, candy popcorn, or if really hungry, could walk next door to a small corner café, and order up a big, cooked-to-order hamburger or cheeseburger and an order of fries, and be made to feel like a king while you ate and watched the movie. For re-entry, you simply told the ticket agent what you were doing, where you were going, and then when you came back, he would wave you on through. Made you feel like a big shot, when there was a line, and you ambled your way to the front, and he recognized you and waved you in.

It was on one such afternoon that Thomas, Myra's son, went to the movies with a friend of his. As he paid for his ticket, the ticket agent took his money, and waved him through. As Thomas was walking up the stairs, a voice from within the white area was heard saying, "There's that white nigger." Thomas, unknowing the comment was meant for him, walked on. When he went home later, his mother was sitting on the front porch. As he approached her he sat on the stoop, and with his head low, he asked his mother, "Mama, who's a white nigger?" Myra was stunned that he would ask such a question, saying, "Thomas, where on earth did you hear that?" "At the show mama, I heard it." Myra asked him, "When you heard it, who was it that said it, and where were you?" "Walking up the stairs, mama, but everybody heard it." As dreaded as the day was, now was the time Myra had to come clean with Thomas, but in her mind she kept asking herself, "Is he ready?"

Myra began by telling Thomas how much she loved him and how much she depended on him. She made every attempt humanly possible to talk her way around the inevitable, but it was not doing a bit of good, Thomas wanted to know, and he wanted to know now. She had led the horse to the trough, and now, he had to drink!" Thomas, you are my baby, "I brought you into the world, and I have never regretted it. When I was very young, I had a friend, a white

Where Cotton Grows

friend, and I liked him a lot. This white friend was a boy, about my same age, and even though your granny and granddaddy did not want us talking, we were friends, and in our hearts and minds it did not matter. That white boy became my close friend, and even though, in my heart, I knew, that reality would never allow me and him to ever be anything more than friends; we did our best to create a friendship that would never be broken. And that's how you came to be, baby. Your daddy is the young white boy which was my best friend. Your granddaddy has never forgiven me, has never forgotten what I did, and he never will, but that does not mean he doesn't love you. Thomas, at a time in the future, when I feel you are ready, I will tell you the rest, and I promise you, I will tell you who your father is, but you are too young now, and it is better you do not know everything at this time. You must trust me, and believe that I have your best interest at heart." And with a nod of his head, and questions in his eyes, respecting his mother, he arose, walked into the house, and got ready for bed. Myra sat quietly on the porch, feeling as if the burden of guilt would never be lifted from her heart and soul. She bowed her head, and again asked God to forgive her, then sat quietly for a little longer, finally giving way to sleepy eyes, when she arose and walked through the screen door, turning to lock it, and then the wooden door, and on walking into her room and preparing for bed.

～ ～ ～

Cars were everywhere. It seemed the mechanical age of automobiles would put to rest every other mode of transportation. Everyone had a car or truck, with exception of most coloreds. Cars cost money, and if you didn't have it, you surely couldn't own it. So, most of the coloreds stayed with the tried and true, the mule. In Greensboro, it was usually the coloreds who you would see on most afternoons riding up and down streets in wagons pulled by mules, and the drivers hollering, "Peanuts, peanuts, for sale", "fresh vegetables, tomatoes, peas, roasting ears, fresh potatoes." It was a poor man's dollar, and made by poor man's sweat and tears. The mules would be so exhausted it seemed they could hardly pull the load, with lather of sweat all over them, and looking nearly ready to drop. Dogs would chase the wagons, bark at the mules' hooves, trying to intimidate then, or scare them. It worked at times, and the drivers would nearly lose control and dump their loads, causing the white children to laugh and make slurs. Not an easy life at all.

~ ~ ~

Tommy, for some time, had something he wanted to get off his chest, and to get this done, he had to see Myra. So, on an afternoon, after he left work, he walked around town, hoping he would see her at the café, but when he arrived he learned she had already left. Making his way to her home through the mesh of streets, mostly dirt, on the hill, he found her, where he had always found her, sitting on her front porch in a rocker shelling peas. As he approached, she recognized him, and he stopped at the gate, asking permission to come and sit on the porch and speak with her for a while. Responding that he could, Tommy opened the gate with caution and care as it was getting old and in need of repair. He sat in the chair nearest her, and this time he looked her straight in the eye, and said. "Myra, I owe you, I owe you." Looking puzzled, Myra answered, "And how would you owe me?" "I have owed you for a long time, and the time to pay up is here. You have been faithful, silent, nonjudgmental, and a good mother and I owe you, Myra. Thomas is mine, we both know it. I would like to contribute to his raising, and help him through school. I have a job, and I can pay, and will pay. You no longer need to bear the burden alone. It took two to do what we did, so I want to take responsibility. Please do not refuse my help, I owe it to you." As Tommy gave her one hundred dollars in hand, Myra dropped her head and cried, and with tears in her eyes, she looked up at him and said, "Tommy, as a woman, I have always loved you, both as a friend, and as a man, and even though in my heart, what happened, produced something so wonderful, we both made a serious mistake. This little boy has questions, and someday those questions are going to have to be answered. Since his daddy cannot be there, and all, I will have to be the one to answer them. If only I had someone to help share in that with me." Tommy looked at Myra and said, "Myra, he's part mine, and if you need me, you know I will be there. I have never tried to hide this, and I never will." Oh; how Myra wished in her mind this could be only the truth, but deep in her heart, she knew the day would come when she felt that Tommy would deny Thomas, for fear of jeopardizing his regular life. For Myra, the burden would forever be hers.

~ ~ ~

It was a happy day. Thomas turned eighteen years old, and to enjoy the celebration was his mother, Myra, his granny and his granddad, who now was well into his seventies, as was his granny. A pretty

Mike Reed

cake, homemade ice-cream, and presents from family and friends surrounded Thomas. He was on cloud nine. To make things better, Myra learned that Thomas had himself a girlfriend, a little girl whom he had met at church and whose father was a deacon in the Mount Moriah congregation. Indeed, this was a day to give thanks for. Thomas was eighteen, a young man and now, a Christian girl….. what more could you pray for?

Among the gifts on the table, lay two small envelopes, the first bearing the writing of a man, with the name "Thomas, Happy Birthday", written on it. Inside the envelope were two crisp ten dollar bills. What one earth? "Who did this?" asked Thomas. Everyone at the table was wide-eyed and surprised, for no one had any idea. How this could have gotten here and no one recognized it? The other envelope, plain, and written on the outside, "Happy Birthday, Thomas, Angels are watching over you." No signature, but the distinct hint of an aromatic perfume was present. Who sent this, but it was evident, no one knew and no one had seen anyone that could have delivered it. Inside the envelope, was a note, which read, "From heaven fall's the rain, but be not afraid, for you feel only the tears of joy from God's angels as they watch over you?" Underneath the inscription was a crisp one hundred dollar bill, and on the reverse of the note another inscription that read, "Thomas, the path is straight, be proud of who you are, and what you are, and I will be watching you." Silence could be felt all over the room. Who did this…..there were no signatures, and yet, they knew exactly who to send it to, and how to get it there without being seen. Thomas smiled, turned and looked at his mother and said, "Oh! I believe in angels, I've had one close by me since birth."

The seasons of Greensboro would come and go, but little changed in this small community. Time seemed to stand still, yet people grew older. Tommy found himself promoted to bank officer, while Myra waited tables, and struggled to maintain her lifestyle. Thomas worked part time in the café as a dish-washer, helping his mother and grandfather. Myra's mother stayed home, cooking, cleaning and maintaining the home life. The house needed paint, the fence was in dire need of repair, roses bloomed, honeysuckle climbed fence posts, the dogs continued to lazily lay about the yard, and the birds continued to nest in the trees that surrounded the house. On the hill, the lifestyle was that of lower middle class poverty, never reflecting the inner ambitions of its inhabitants.

The fields were almost bare from harvest. It had been a bumper crop year, there were smiles on the streets, with bragging of how good the year had been. Merchants noticed an upswing in sales, new clothes were being purchased, most credit tabs were paid, and an economic boost was the conversation at hand. The gins were working twenty four/seven, employing more than ever before. Supply was having a difficult time keeping up with demand. The rail yard was visible with nothing but bales of cotton stacked high and wide. Cotton buyers were steady. The local hotel had few rooms for rent, and most boarding houses were packed to capacity. There was even an increase in birthrate. Churches were growing in number, and on the hill, singing grew louder. The preaching seemed unending; there was much to be thankful for. Myra and Thomas were regular attendees at the Mount Moriah Church, where she had gone since childhood. Most all members were either family or close friends, having known them her entire life.

In Greensboro, it seemed the same. Tommy and his family were regulars at the First Baptist Church. Like Myra, he had attended here for as long as he could remember. First, it was children's choir, the adult choir, and an active member of the young men's Sunday school Class. The faces he met each Sunday morning were those of people he had known his entire life. Even the dog that lay beneath the steps on Sunday mornings waiting to greet the parishioners as they went to and fro was familiar.

Finally, word came. A suspect had been questioned in the murder of the colored man found on the railroad tracks. Talk grew rampant: who was it? The matter was kept quiet, so as not to "taint" the case; however, speculation from several who were considered to be "in the know" alluded to a certain and well respected man in town. Everyone, over and over, in every conversation that occurred said, "I just do not understand, why? Why?" Of course, in the course of conversation, and considering speculation, mostly all conversations became gossip, and within a short time, the names of a couple of people surfaced as prospective suspects. Who was it?

Gossip was rampant, speculation surfaced in every conversation, and still no one had any idea of who had been brought in for questioning. However, there was a suspect. The sheriff was saying nothing, even when asked by the closest of friends. Word was not going to leak out in this administration, no matter what. Too much time had lapsed, too many were accusing so little had been done, and nothing or no one was going to jeopardize this case. All three deputies had been given explicit instruction to say absolutely nothing with regard to the case, or anyone having anything in any way to do with it. Sounded like they had a hot prospect, but then again, was it

Where Cotton Grows

just a ploy to divert attention trying to make everything think they were closing in? Or better yet, were they trying to lure the guilty party or parties out into the open? Time would tell.

∼ ∼ ∼

Miss Jean, as she sat at her desk, gave delivery assignments to the driver who would deliver fuel to the farms that had submitted orders. She always went to work early, usually around seven o'clock in the morning, just to have some time to read the paper, or the latest gardening magazines that lay sprawled everywhere in her office. She was an avid gardener, and it was no secret that she held the distinction of having cutting rights in every yard in Greensboro. You might say, she was the resident gardening expert, and she took great pride in sharing her expertise on the subject with anyone who showed the least of interest.

The driver, loaded, and ready to leave, came into the office once more, in case Miss Jean had any last minute instructions that he might need to take care of. As he entered, Miss Jean was sitting at her desk, reading the weekly paper, and with the raising of an eyebrow, looked at him and said, "Well, looks like we might have someone in mind?" "Hope so", said the driver, "it ain't right they let it go so long:" You know they have an idée who done this and they needs to do something about it." With concern in her eyes, Miss Jean, said, "I'll Suwannee, Frog, you sound like a politician!" "I ain't a politician, Miss Jean, but I do know what's right, and if I say so myself, somebody needs to pay for this, and the white folks know it." Miss Jean never questioned Frog. He was an honest, hard working colored man, who had served the interests of her and her husband for some thirty years. He had had no other job. Frog lived on the hill, as did most of the other colored who worked in and around Greensboro, in a modest, plain frame house that displayed the cracking and peeling of paint. He had raised and supported eight children and a wife on his salary, and now, in his near retirement years, was dreading no longer having to get up in the morning and come to work, and drive the fuel truck for Miss Jean and Mr. Conrad.

The gasoline pump bells rang as the Sheriffs patrol car pulled in to fill up. The attendant went to assist. "Fill'er up.", he was told by the deputy. As the deputy turned and looked toward the coca-cola machine, walking towards it, he looked the office where Miss Jean was sitting and looking out. The deputy waved, and she, waving back, motioned him to come inside. As the deputy entered the office, Miss Jean, from where she was sitting, said, "Well, looks like we got us a suspect?" "Yes, mam", replied the deputy with almost a look of relief on his face. "Anybody we might know, young fella?" asked Miss Jean. "Might, and then might not,", as he replied with a half grin on his face. "Well, I just hope this thing comes to a head before too long. It's not right to sit by, especially if there's someone out there that needs to be dealt with", said Miss Jean. "Oh", said the deputy, "he'll be dealt with, I can assure you of that." Considering the way the deputy had answered and looked while he answered made Miss Jean think it was someone that most would least suspect; but, again, who? Surely the secret wasn't that well kept.

The next day in the local newspaper, there it was, in big bold letters right on the front page, and better yet, center page......"MAN ARRESTED IN DEATH OF RAILROAD MURDER". There it was. It was out, but Who?......Everyone, as they read, scanned like radar guns, trying to find the name of the accused, and then, like being hit in the eye with a big chocolate pie the name Haskell Rhodes appeared. Haskell Rhodes? What on earth? The serious reading began, and throughout town as each person read, no talking, no eating, drinking or anything else was being done, at least until the entire column was consumed, processed, and digested. Questions had to be answered, questions had to be asked, and beyond all else, why?

The suspect was being held temporarily in what everyone referred to as the calaboose, which was located on the back alley, and just across from the café. After being held there for some three days, the Sheriff and legal representatives involved felt that keeping Haskell Rhodes so near, and at an out of the way place, exposing him to the possibilities of would-be danger, was a chance they rather not take, so after a hearing in the local chambers of Judge Cobb, it was decided that Haskell would be removed and placed in the county facility located in the town of Gore City, some 3 miles plus just North of Greensboro. He would be away from the unsolicited opportunities of possible harm, and the temptation of those passing by to taunt and jester would be removed. In small towns, when people went to jail, it was not uncommon for people to ride by at all times of the day and night and yell obscenities and make jabs at those who were incarcerated. Haskell, a middle aged man, white, a farmer, and one who was not known to be anyone of violence, was closed mouth about everything. His lawyer, a local gentleman, low key, and known for his expertise of the law, had visited his client and advised him to remain as silent as possible, allowing no one the opportunity to obtain anything that could be in any way twisted or misconstrued into what might or might not have happened. No chances were being taken.

The county jail was a small brick building, containing some four, small, cramped cells, conveniently located directly behind the courthouse itself. Removal of the prisoner for court appearances would be easy, and convenient. This would allow for decrease of opportunity of possible attempts on Haskell's life. Within a week, the attorneys met with the judge in the chambers and discussed trial proceedings. The district attorney wanted to expedite things, as he felt the people had been held in suspense long enough. He felt the taxpayers did not need to bear the burden of a long and drawn out trial, while the defense argued that his client needed time so as to allow him to extensively research the situation and with his client's help, retrace the events as they had unfolded on the night in question when the man had been killed. Judge Cobb, wanted time to consider the alternatives, and being close friends with both attorneys, made the job no easier for him…he just knew that a trial had to happen, and that justice must be served.

The date was set in a hearing and the lawyers excused preparing their arguments for trial. After many meetings with Haskell Rhodes, Haskell's lawyer was convinced beyond a shadow of a doubt that his client was innocent, but he was not convinced that his client wasn't aware of it. He made his client aware of his options, too. Being guilty of a murder, and having knowledge of one, is two entirely different things. He had to clear his Clients' name, but he also had to find out more, and his client was tight lipped about this.

It was late at night, and Haskell's lawyer sat in his study in his home going over and over in his mind the events which were involved in this case. He just could not, for the life of him, understand why anyone would be so tight-lipped about something like this, especially if his life hung in the balance. What would it prove, what possible gain could one realize from it? There was more meat in this soup, he just had to find it, and he would, because after all, he was a country lawyer, he made his living the hard way, and no way would he give up. It wasn't that he was so close to Haskell, it was because he had principles, and if a man doesn't have principles, then he has nothing. After this was over, he would once again have to return to work, accept more cases, and go on, and no way would this hang over his head!

~ ~ ~

The court room was packed! The bailiff stood beside the door which led through the back way and into the hall, which led also to the judge's chambers. Judge Cobb was a bearded man, in his mid-sixties, weighing about two hundred and fifty pounds, always wearing red suspenders, hair half combed, and who always smoked either a cigar or a pipe, depending on how he felt when he wanted to smoke. He was a even tempered, God fearing man, who came from humble beginnings, and had worked his way through college, and law school. The judge was a family man, and a regular attendee in the over-fifty men's Sunday school class at the First Baptist Church. He took a dim liking to people who used his name in conversation with regard to personal friendships. He aspired to never mix business with pleasure, sometimes succeeding and sometimes not. He was a normal man, who had a rough job, but if he did it, it would be done right, and to the letter of the law. No exceptions!

The judge entered the court room. As he took his right hand, slowly running it through his balding head of hair, he looked over the open court room, then turning left, walked slowly, stepping up two steps and onto the bench where he presided as judge. This was his world, a lonely world, having to separate fact from fiction, personal from professional, and doing always his best to conduct proceedings in a legal and dignified manner. As he sat back into his high-back solid oak swivel chair, he placed his hands on the desk of the bench and drew himself forward. Reaching for his glasses with his hand, he placed them on his face, looking down to review the documents before him. After what seemed to be an eternity, he looked up, and peering at both lawyers he asked, "Gentlemen, are we ready to proceed?" Both lawyers almost unanimously replied, "Yes, your honor." The judge then exclaimed, "Mr. Rhodes, how do you plead?" Standing, and almost trembling, Haskell Rhodes answered, "Not guilty, your honor."

The trial proceeds the first day for some six and one-half hours. The prosecution as well as the defense questioned many prospective witnesses; doing their best to justify their theories with facts they perceived to surround the case. In the courtroom, people came as if attending church on Sunday morning. It was a show as well as a court trial. Greensboro and Sumner County rarely held such as this. It was both newsworthy and made for good conversation. The courthouse, which had been built during the late eighteen hundreds, provided segregated seating; the colored populous sat in the upstairs, or balcony, area and the whites sat below in the main open court room. Throughout the opening day of arguments children viewing from the upstairs could be seen leaning on the balcony restraints, peering into the downstairs audience. Many felt this to be uncalled for, as in their opinions it was distracting. The balcony was always seated to capacity.

The trial made its way through the first week, mostly establishing scenarios and the whereabouts of Haskell Rhodes at the time of the death of colored man that had been found laying on the railroad tracks in the bend, underneath the overhanging branches of the shady trees situated along the tracks leading from and into town. The railroad company, at least twice yearly, had crews cut back the overgrowth, but at the time of this occurring, this had not happened. The newspaper printed repetitive news items about the trial, and even on a couple of occasions special editions were printed to keep the public apprised of the proceedings. Several felt the trial was a hoax, just a way to appease the coloreds for what they considered to be an attack on their race. Others wanted the course of justice to proceed.

During the second week, neither lawyer felt any closer to the conclusion than when the whole thing started. Judge Cobb, by mid-afternoon on a Thursday asked the lawyers to approach the bench. Rather than openly in court chastise them for frivolous questioning, he chose to do it at close range, and where no one could hear him. "Gentlemen, enough marble playing, get down to business, or we go to recess." The lawyers, turned, walked back to their seats, and sat down.

Throughout a maze of witnesses the prosecution felt confident he had placed Haskell Rhodes at the crime scene, but not without a few holes in his story. Haskell Rhodes worked for the railroad, and his being anywhere near the tracks, whether business or not, and depending on what he said he was doing, as long as it was considered business, no one could totally prove him doing wrong. He needed more. The defense, argued his client was totally innocent, had no knowledge of this crime, was nowhere near the tracks when this happened; therefore could not be a party to such. Someone was lying, or was they?

Over the next few days, as the trial neared completion, both lawyers argued unceasing as to the guilt and innocence of the accused. The last five witnesses, held in seclusion by the defense with the knowledge of the Prosecution, were yet to be heard. The prosecution, having to be aware of all witnesses and the testimony thereof, did not seem worried that the forth-coming witnesses would be detrimental to his case for getting the guilt verdict, so, almost with a smirk; he allowed it to go forward.

The defense lawyer, called the first prime witness, the wife of Haskell Rhodes. Mrs. Rhodes testified that her husband had worked the day in question, which he had arrived home as always and almost at the exact same time. She stated, under oath, that he wore overalls, brogans, khaki shirt, just as he usually always did. There was absolutely nothing about this day that was different than any other day, with the exception that a man had been killed, and within two hundred and fifty yards of their home. She swore, under oath, that her husband, when he arrived home, was not suspicious, and did not display any signs of having a hard fought fight. The prosecution cross examined asking if she was absolutely, positively, sure that everything she had just said was in fact the truth. Mrs. Rhodes replied, "Yes sir". "What did you cook for supper, on this evening, Mrs. Rhodes", asked the prosecuting lawyer. "The usual sir, Corn bread, sweet tea, ham hocks in greens, purple hull peas, fresh tomatoes and fresh onions". "May I sit at your table Mrs. Rhodes? You have indeed made me hungry, and I believe I could eat right now." Laughter filled the court room. "Yes, sir, you surely may. Just bring your wife, sir." More laughter lifted to the rafter in the old building. "Okay, Mrs. Rhodes", said the prosecutor, "so you are saying, without any doubt, that your husband is like clockwork each and every day, am I correct?" "Yes sir, within reason, and allowing a minute or two here and there, yes, sir, he most assuredly is." "Well, Mrs. Rhodes, we are in a very uncomfortable situation here, because I'm doing my best to prove your husband killed this man, so my question to you, madam, is, if your husband didn't kill him, then who did?" As her face flushed, Mrs. Rhodes said, "Sir, I have no idea."

The defense attorney approached the stand, and with his right hand, he placed it on Mrs. Rhodes hand, telling her, "Mrs. Rhodes, we know he's innocent, and so do you, so don't worry, everything will be all right." The lawyer turned and faced the jury. As he stood looking straight into the eyes of all twelve jurors, including two alternate jurors who sat close by, he just stood there for what seemed like an eternity, and then all of a sudden said, "Well, who killed him?" "It wasn't Haskell Rhodes." The lawyer then walked toward the jurors, picking up a stick that had been entered as an exhibit. "Ladies and gentlemen of the jury, in good conscience, and considering the evidence submitted herein, I just for the life of me, as a trained servant of jurisprudence, cannot come to the conclusion that this man, in any way, had anything to do with this murder. It seems to me, he serves the cause of a scapegoat, caught up in a trap that unless we help to free him from, will die for a crime that he did not commit. This trial has got to conclude with the guilty party, but so far, we have no guilty party." Mrs. Rhodes was dismissed and asked to step down.

The other four witnesses called were the sheriff, his lead deputy, the owner of the back alley café, and a county supervisor. Each, taking the stand in the course of events, all answering questions from both lawyers, were dismissed and allowed to take their respective seats. Judge Cobb recessed court for the day at four o'clock in the afternoon, telling everyone, court would resume at eight o'clock in the morning.

By early morning of the next day, the sheriff, his deputies, the judge, both lawyers, and the court reporter, all assembled in the judge's chambers for an emergency meeting called by the judge himself. "Gentlemen, it appears, that during the course of events, a prisoner being held in the county jail, has submitted a statement, under oath, that the gentleman in question of whom we have on trial for this murder is indeed an innocent man and at this time I would like to introduce this statement as evidence and declare this a mistrial." It was done, Haskell Rhodes was free, and as he met his wife, with hugs and kisses, and not without tears, they both departed the court room for their home.

~ ~ ~

Everyone was up in arms. Surely such a mockery of a trial was only a ploy to bring someone to trial, and then hold a kangaroo court, only to release them based on insufficient evidence. There was some who found this very uneasy feeling, and no longer felt the ease of exclusion as they once had thought.

Another arrest was made, another trial held, and yet another long, lengthy court battle ensued but in the end it was realized the prisoner in the county jail had indeed told the truth, and justice was finally served. The colored man, who had been killed on the tracks, was killed by a husband who had caught him seeing his wife. The man who had been killed worked for the town of Greensboro as a garbage collector. The man, who killed him, was a long time respected citizen of the community, a colored man, but whose wife was some twenty years younger that was he. The man who committed the crime was the local colored undertaker. The headlines still made front page news, but rarely were there special editions as the trial ensued.

∽ ∽ ∽

Summer gave way to fall, the leaves began to die, change colors, and become strewn throughout the yards of Greensboro. School children picked up odd jobs after school raking leaves into large piles and burning them, a way of making extra money for much needed spending change to attend the theater matinees on Saturday afternoons, and ride the range with Roy Rogers and Dale Evans.

Miss Jean passed the corner grocery store, pedal to the metal, but she wasn't worried. No policeman in his right mind would dare mess with the white hairs. She could prove it too. Just one call to Conrad, that's all! Miss Jean had been the recipient of several speeding tickets, only to present them to Conrad, and with little effort, even if it meant settling a long overdue debt strictly between business acquaintances, the citation would surely be forgotten.

Miss Nellie, a close friend of Miss Jean's was also a prominent lady in Greensboro. Miss Nellie's husband had had the good fortune of amassing a great deal of wealth in the automotive industry. Their life together was childless, so most children in town, as with Miss Jean, were considered their adoptive family. Miss Nellie worked with her husband, as did Miss Jean. They both kept the books, taking care of the office work, and running the daily operations while her husband tended to the more needed technical aspects of their business. A young state policeman once stopped Miss Nellie

Mike Reed

en-route to another town, on a business trip for her husband. Being on time constraints, Miss Nellie, as Miss Jean, had little or no regard for the speed laws. As the young policeman sounded the siren and turned on the squad cars lights to pull her over, stepped from his vehicle and approached the car Miss Nellie was driving. Miss Nellie, rolling down her window, exclaimed, "Son, what can I do for you?" The policeman replied, "Lady, do you have any idea how fast you were driving?" Miss Nellie replied, "No, I don't." As the young officer wrote out the citation for Miss Nellie, she placed her hand on the door, and asked, "Son, do you know who I am?" The officer replied, "No, mam, I do not." Miss Nellie proceeded to explain who she was telling him of her and her husband and their businesses. The young officer ripped the citation from the booklet he had written it from and handed it to her. He again reminded her to hold the speed down, and observe the posted speed limit. As he walked away Miss Nellie, with tight lips, sat there impatiently, as the officer walked back to his vehicle to put away the ticket book, and drive away. After a while, the young officer got out, and walked back up to Miss Nellie's car, and as she sat there in the same position as when he had left her, he asked, "Mam, can I help you?" Miss Nellie replied, "I'm waiting for the other ticket." The young officer, looking stunned, asked, "What other ticket?" Miss Nellie replied, "Well, I've got to come back this way."

∽ ∽ ∽

On another very sunny day in Greensboro, Miss Nellie, long after her husband had passed away, had taken her car to a local service station, to have it serviced, and washed. The attendant, having known her from previous business, offered to drive her back home and bring the car back for servicing and washing. They promised once they had finished, they would return her car, and not in a long time frame. This satisfied Miss Nellie, so she was taken home. After approximately two hours had passed, Miss Nellie noticed her car was back in the driveway, so as before, she walked out and gave it the once over. Within fifteen minutes or so, she had taken the car back to the service station, complaining to the owner and attendants that it was not clean and she wanted it cleaned as it had always been. The owner, who by now had emerged from the station, was confronted by Miss Nellie. "Miss Nellie, your car is clean, I know for a fact, I saw them wash and clean it!" Miss Nellie replied, "No, sir, it is not clean, you have not washed the underside of it." The owner, not wanting to cause anymore of a scene looked at Miss Nellie and said, "Miss Nellie, not a soul in this town is going to ever look up under this car, to see if has been washed or not." Miss Nellie, taking the cigarette from her mouth with her right hand, looked at the owner and replied, "No, they don't, and no one in town looks at my rear end either, but I still wash it!"

~ ~ ~

Greensboro was under the blanket of a beautiful fall. There's something about the changing of seasons in the country and small country towns that brings out the best in people. It's a festive time, a time of giving, the renewing of old acquaintances, visiting the shut-ins, and putting on a new face. If only we could continue this throughout the entire year. Greensboro was no exception; we had our blood bound enemies. We just never chose to talk about them, thinking if we never brought the subject up, they would never emerge from the closets they were kept in.

Myra became ill with the flu, being unable to work in the café. She stayed home, and Thomas took up the slack for her, waiting tables, taking orders, and running errands. Running errands was something he liked because it allowed him to walk to the other street, Main Street, and see the white people and how they conducted themselves. Thomas began to change. He became more of a man, and a nice young man. More and more were his features of the Caucasian race. His nose, an even blend of both mother and father, and his skin were almost that of a not so darkened tan. He could have easily passed for Hispanic, or possibly, lower European. Myra was more proud of him than ever. She had no intentions of him ever staying here as an adult. Her dream was for him to go to college and move to someplace like Chicago, or even New York. Her dreams for her son reached far beyond the cotton fields of Greensboro, Mississippi. She knew that for him there was no future here, and when he left, so would she. She could accept that anymore than what already had occurred between her and Tommy would ever blossom, so, instead of remaining in the scars of childhood, she would also leave and leave the memories and past behind them.

~ ~ ~

The depression had left such an impact on Greensboro. People were still trying to recover. Of course, people here, during the depression ate, mainly because they raised their food at home, shopping in the stores for very little other than the staples required. Clothes were mostly homemade, and rarely, if ever, did anyone have automobiles. Only recently had the emergence of the automobile found its way into mainstream Greensboro. Few could afford them, and if there was money to buy a vehicle, then surely it could be used for a better cause. Wages were almost at giveaway prices. Sawmills, and plants, along with farming were the industries of profession. Most people rarely had that. Crops were made and practically given away. Sharecroppers were cheated, and overcharged a lot of the time. Depression in Greensboro was time sadness, but underneath laid the hope for a better way. Soon it would come, but for some, it would be too late.

In Greensboro, some were so short on cash on hand; they slowly sold away their inheritances, dollar by dollar, and acre by acre. The sadness of losing what had been fought for with blood, sweat, and tears were almost unbearable. One prominent local family's oldest daughter, who had married and moved away, had been consumed so by the stock market crash she chose jumping from an ocean liner at sea, rather than face the inevitable upon her return to her home. She was buried in Greensboro Cemetery alongside her grandparents. A sad reminder of how much was lost in just a blink of an eye.

～ ～ ～

Tommy became engaged to a local girl, the daughter of a grocery store owner. Although until recent years he had not really noticed her, all of a sudden she became a driving force in his life. She was educated, a local teacher, and very active in the Methodist Church. Tommy, for years now, so it seemed, had not noticed the young man walking around town that he had fathered. One afternoon, as Tommy was leaving the bank, Thomas walked up to him, and asked if he could make a withdrawal. Tommy, not recognizing him at first, said yes, but that he was on his way home, it was closing time. Not until Tommy, took the withdrawal slip from Thomas did he realize who he was. All he could do was look at him, and ask him if he knew who he was. Thomas said that he had heard, but wasn't sure. Tommy told him he was his father, shook his hand, and as Thomas smiled, turned and walked to the door; Tommy thought to himself, he saw a resemblance of his father in Thomas' face. Until now, Tommy was not really aware of the man his son had become and was becoming. He never discussed him, or Myra.

"Here she is all gussied up, smelling like the Delta Queen, I wonder how much the ole girls had to drink today" Asked a bystander on the street. Everyone in Greensboro knew she was a closet drinker. Usually she was present at weddings, always loud, never obnoxious, but always in front of you. She was always there; either helping serve or working the crowd. If she heard it, whatever was said, within fifteen minutes it was old news. She was the social graces representative. Her linage was from prominent southern heritage, cotton farmers, who, if had have ever found out this was to have been her fate would have rolled over in their graves. She had the eyes of an eagle, which, with the smell of vapors on her breath or not, could spot you and call you by name from one end of the street to the other. She bought very little and borrowed a lot. She was a lady and loved beyond blame by all who knew her. The poor benefited from her charity, the churches prospered from her gifts, and to those who would see her on the streets, you were always greeted by a smile, and a kind word of encouragement.

The line to Mr. Jason's counter in the local pool hall was like a revolving door. Hamburgers and cheeseburgers were a dime each, and cokes were a nickel. There was no long wait for a chance at playing one of the regulars in a game of eight ball, or even nine-ball. The table covering was worn and frayed, but a lot of nickels were won and lost in the course of daily challenges dared and accepted. Mr. Jason had been a Greensboro resident since birth. He was one of the first babies born shortly after the city was named. The jukebox played those old honky-tonk songs, and for a nickel. Posters on the walls, both taped or hung over the booths, told of wrestling matches that had been scheduled at the local community center. If a guy was patient enough, sooner or later he could find his way to a pint of Old Crow, or even some good ole homemade moonshine, and for a price to die for, usually between two and three dollars. Of course, if caught, you got a one night pass for free room and board in the calaboose, and if it was filled to capacity, then it meant you were a guest of the county, and Gore City, here you come. The point was, not to get caught. Rarely was this the case. Most of the police, businessmen in town, sheriff, and supervisors all at one time or another participated in the purchase of under the table thirst-quenchers.

Over time, rumors ran rampant that more went on in the pool hall than just pool, but that was usually the idle time passing of ladies who had nothing better to do than gossip. If you wanted an argument on where things happened, you might want to consider the Masonic Hall. If nothing ever goes on there, then why is it, they never allow visitors inside, all the men wear white bib aprons, they always meet upstairs if there are windows on the lower level, they march around in a circle, and they always have guards posted everywhere as if something's going on inside that is clandestine? Makes you think, doesn't it? You hear stories of riding a goat, but if that's really all that goes on, how do they keep the goat from messing up the floor during one of those meetings. The boys in Greensboro timed the meetings over a period of time, and not a one of them ever said the meetings were over before midnight. Something strange happening, and most all of these men are supposed to be respectable citizens. What's odder is that every single one of them has a wife who knows exactly where they, and usually they are beaming with joy, when they kiss them, sending them off to one of the meetings. Word has since come to Greensboro assuring the townspeople it goes on in every town. For the longest time, the young men of Greensboro thought the men met and told fishing lies, and maybe passed around a magazine or two, but this is strictly hearsay.

Days in Greensboro began early in the morning around five o'clock. There were chores to do, and plenty of them, never lacking for something else, just in case you beat the record and finished early. Firewood, a must, especially for those who depended on wood burning fireplaces or stoves, and in many cases, the meals were cooked on these stoves which also provided the main source of heat in the winter. Cooking breakfast on one of these stoves, for the ladies of Greensboro must have been an undertaking of home economic ingenuity. Frying eggs and bacon or ham were easy, it was the biscuits that seemed to be the miracle. Thank God, we were born boys!

Helping feed livestock was a man's world. It meant trudging through the elements at an almost unforgiving hour, usually before the sun ever arose, and usually down a path behind the house to a dark barn, with the smell of fresh dropped cow dung and whatever else that may be laying around. If there was no electricity, it meant carrying a kerosene lantern with you, safeguarding it to never let go out, and for sure never letting it topple over, for fear of starting a fire, that most likely if had started, would have never been put out, because fire hydrants were few and far between. The best you could do and count on in instances like this, if it ever happened, was the well, and for those who endured this task, drawing that much water, as fast as you would have needed it would have either killed you, or made you let the barn burn. Feeding the livestock was first and foremost. Hay to all, and if you had it, either oats or corn. Everyone tried to keep a cow with a calf because it meant fresh milk.

~ ~ ~

The Fourth of July in Greensboro was a special time. It always meant that if the day occurred during the week, you were off. It further meant picnics, homemade ice cream, and for the teenagers and adults, it meant the Fourth of July street dance which, since the beginning, had always been held on Main Street. Usually, a band was hired, (mostly locals), who would play and sing, while people would dance until at least ten o'clock at night. The dance never started before the sun went down. All the young people made it a point to come, and made an evening of it. A lot of marriages were formulated and carried through with, all because of the Fourth of July street dance and picnic. It was a happy time for all. Greensboro would grow, and along with growth, it meant that, as some would say, the personality of the town would change, and not be as it had always been. Such thinking is dangerous, and can cause the demise of settlements, and has happened time and again, but not here in this time capsule where everyone is happy, and content. The people of Greensboro were determined to make their town a better place. With people like Miss Jean and Conrad, it would always have a chance. This was their home, they let you know it. The merchants always stood solid as a body of people, supporting events and helping wherever and whenever they could. No one in Greensboro went without, if it was something they really needed. The people took care of each other, it had always been like that, and if they had anything to do with it, it would always be like that.

∾ ∾ ∾

The fog lay over the small town like a shroud. On the ponds and creek beds it appeared as if steam rising from a hot pot of water. The sun began to peek through the trees slowly burning off the morning mist. As cars made their way through the streets to places of business, and people scurried about morning chores, in the distance the barking of dogs became muffled by the whistle blowing at the local plant to mark the start of the days work. In the rail yard, horses pulling wagons and drays trudged along the rows placing the outbound cargo of cotton and other items in places for easy loading and unloading. The morning train would be puffing into town with hours and this meant fast work and sweat laden brows.

The streets, back alleys and paths became filled with children making their way to the school, located atop the hill that separated Greensboro from the hill, each laden with books, carrying usually a small lunch to help them through the day. Life was simple, uncomplicated, and yet, many felt this was the world, the only world they knew. To read about far away places, in the minds of many, was a waste. Few would ever leave.

Myra, still pretty, made her way to the café, to begin another day. For her, this was the world, her world. She still wondered about Tommy, and the day they met. Her memory always recalled that day at the hole. She had dreamed in the stillness of the night about all the what-ifs, and how it would and could have been. But, she knew, reality would never let her go beyond her dreams, for this indeed was another world, a world of reality. Through the years, Myra had accepted requests from suitors to attend church functions, picnics, and celebrations, but she had never allowed it to go beyond friendship. Several had attempted to woo her and win her hand, never allowing herself to let go of her memories. In Greensboro, such as she had dreamed of would never be a reality; the times would not allow it. She held strong to her faith and her to her son. Thomas, although he knew about Tommy, had never questioned his mother. If the subject was ever implied, it soon became a closed matter. Thomas, in his logic, could not understand, although he tried. He wanted his mother to be happy, but as days gave way to years, he noticed she relied more on her privacy, always changing the subject. She was now in her mid thirties, knowing and feeling that life had passed her by.

Tommy now resided in the old Watkins home, near the home of his parents, but located on another street. It was near the bank, and easy walking. He had bought a car, but rarely drove it, always walking. From time to time each would catch a glimpse of the other, never allowing themselves to go beyond a look and a nod, with a seldom, "good morning." Tommy turned the corner onto Main Street, and walked face first right into Myra. This time, unlike others, he stopped, with his hand tipped his hat, and smiled.

Myra smiled and said, "Good morning, sir." As she walked past, Tommy turned slightly and stopped. As he paused, he turned and called, "Myra?" Myra, turning and looking back replied, "Yes sir, Mr. Tommy." Tommy walked to her and said, "Myra, there is no need to sir me, we know each other, and besides we are the same age almost." She lowered her eyes, and without thinking replied, "Yes, sir." Smiling, Tommy touched her hand and said, "Myra, it's me."

As the two parted, Tommy walked on to the bank to begin his daily work, and Myra left thinking, which quickly gave way to a slight smile. Somehow, in the tone of his voice, and the look in his eyes, she realized and knew that it was she he had noticed, and in the right moment of time had come to realize he still saw in her the young girl he had met so many years prior. As she walked on to the café, she began to hum and the smile grew wider.

~ ~ ~

Sirens were heard all over town, the police were making their way to Main Street. Talking and yelling, as they ran past people crowded in front of the bank. An attempted robbery, spoiled by an unexpected off duty policeman, had occurred. No one was allowed inside the bank, the president didn't want anything tampered with until bank officials arrived. Before anything could be accomplished they needed the federal people to come and assess exactly how much, if any, had been taken, but rumor was there had been no money taken, just an exchange of gunfire, which ended in two people being wounded, the gunman, and an employee of the bank, who, in a moment of fear and bravery had leapt from a side office onto the would be robber, knocking him to the floor, followed by a life-threatening brawl all over the floor of the bank. There on the floor of the bank, the shiny, hard white tiles lay Tommy and the perpetrator. The perpetrator was unconscious, while Tommy was conscious but bleeding quite heavily from his side. Surveying the scene, several of the women working in the bank rushed to Tommy and tried to calm him. Seeing the wound they prayed they could hopefully stop the bleeding. They placed wet compresses against his starched white shirt, and sat with him, holding his hand until the doctor could come, who by now was running down the street, medical bag in hand, and telling everyone to get out of his way. For an older man, the doctor sprinted as if a teenager in a cross country race, determination on his face, and a sense of compassion and caring in his eyes.

As the doctor managed his way into the bank, there on the floor before him lay Tommy and the perpetrator. Those inside, first directing him to Tommy, as by now, blood was on the floor, and not having knowledge of the extent of damage, he went to work. As the doctor assessed Tommy's wounds, he told some men standing nearby to pick him up and bring him to the clinic, which they quickly did. Running up Main Street, blood stains on his shirt, and not knowing if he was in grave danger or not, the men ran like ants carrying a large crumb of bread. Once in the clinic and on the examination table the doctor, telling his nurse to clear the room, prepared to examine Tommy and assess the damage and what could be done.

Nearly two hours had passed, when the doctor emerged, unsmiling, and telling those in the family who were present of Tommy's condition. He had been shot, once in the left side, just below his lung. He was sure the bullet had come near the heart, but didn't think it had nicked or pierced his heart. He was in serious condition. This was not a hospital, and even though he was a surgeon he really wasn't equipped to conduct major surgical procedures here in Greensboro. He could, he thought, get Tommy through this but it was left up to the family. Realizing Tommy's condition, and with him now unconsciously lying there on the table, Tommy's mother and father decided to allow the doctor to treat him. The doctor had assisted Tommy's mother in his birth, and no one in town medically knew him better. Tommy lay on the table for some time, until the doctor completed as thorough an examination as he could. Then after reassessing what he had done to save Tommy, he moved him to a room and placed him in a bed. Strict instructions were given to monitor Tommy continuously until signs of any improvement were noticed. So with family present and the attendance of the nurse, the long tiresome wait began. The days passed, then the night, and still no signs of improvement and no awareness. Tommy lay still and quiet in his bed, his mother holding his hand and his father standing close by.

The word circulated throughout the town, soon reaching the back alleys and the café where Myra worked. When Myra learned of the incident, she took off her apron, threw it on the table she was cleaning and ran as fast as she could to the clinic. Being colored, she could only enter the clinic through the back way, so as she made her way through the halls and into the area where blacks were permitted to go, she stopped at the desk and asked about Tommy. The nurse, asking her to state her business and need to know, Myra just sank back and said, "He's someone I know, and I want to check on him." The nurse, with a solemn look, raised her head, and said to Myra, "Coloreds are not allowed in the white part of the hospital unless you work here." Myra asked the nurse, to please let her see him but she refused, repeating what she had already told her. Myra needed to know, she had to know. She did not want him to die, without her having an opportunity to tell him goodbye. Although few in town knew it, Tommy was her son's father, and although she would never make it public, she had to see him, he was her friend, had always been her friend.

Myra stood outside the clinic, with tears in her eyes, waiting for anyone to come out that might have been in visiting Tommy. She stood there for over an hour before finally Tommy's mother walked out, and Myra walked up to her, stood straight, and asked her, "Miss, how is Tommy?" Tommy's mother said he was holding his own, but that he still was not out of the woods and it would be a long time before he was. As Myra turned and started walking back to the street, Tommy's mother, called to her, "Young lady, do I know you? How do you know Tommy?" Myra, turned and smiled and replied, "Miss, he is my friend. We have known each other since we were little." "Well", replied Tommy's mother, "would you like to go in and see him for a minute?" As Myra entered the room, Tommy's father, eyes wide, looked up, and as he saw his wife he noticed the almost unnoticeable shaking of her head acknowledging to him that it was okay. Myra walked to the bed looked down at Tommy and began to cry, and then softly, almost quietly, began to pray. She placed her hand on his, and looked at his face. Faint tears welled up in her eyes as she knew her time was almost up. Placing her hand to her face, as if to hold back emotion, she kissed her hand, then again removed it, placing it on Tommy's hand. As Myra turned from the bed, and to the door of the room, Tommy's mother walked with her. As Myra looked back one more time, he eyes caught a glimpse of the man who was Thomas' father, and silently to her, she said, "Good-bye, Tommy, the kiss was from your son and me."

The walk was laborious for Myra as she made her way back to the café. Along the way, she passed Miss Polly's Tea Room, an established eatery, serving the finest in southern cuisine. Today, it

Mike Reed

smelled, from the aromatic subtle aromas, as the door opened and closed from people coming and going, as if it was a day of Tuscan food, prepared as no other could. Miss Polly, a tried and true lady of the old south prided herself in a touch above, when it came to cooking. Going to her Tea Room meant eating, whether you had the appetite or not. If you didn't eat, there would always the chance that your stomach would kill you, and then tell God you died. The Tea Room had been renovated from what in years past had been an old furniture store and a grocery store. The décor provided an atmosphere of dining in another country, where one could experience and savor the origin of whatever food she would prepare. An experience tried and tested by almost everyone, which is why they continued to return time and again. There was always more than just dining. While you waited, you could always explore the different antiques and paintings that were displayed throughout the dining area. Greensboro might have been a little out of the way town, but we had our etiquette too.

~ ~ ~

Thomas appeared dressed neat and as if prepared to hop the train and leave. Myra from the kitchen, peering through the window where food was passed to and from, smiled, winked, then made her way around the end and out between the walls partition that connected the middle section of the café to the side walls. "Hey, Mama", said Thomas. "Hey baby, how's mama's boy?" "Just fine Mama, cleaned up and ready to go apply for a part-time job." "Okay, son, but remember, you be home on time, you have things to do, and I don't want you out carousing, especially at night." As he left the café, he turned and winked at her, just to let her know, she had been heard, and her word heeded. He was a good boy, respectful, well taught, and hard working. Whatever he could do to help out, he was more than willing to do. After all, it was she who had sacrificed for him, and now, it was his turn to do for her. He loved his Mama!

~ ~ ~

It was Thursday, and that meant the weekly newspaper would be on the racks this afternoon shortly after two o'clock. Usually, there was always a race, when the paperboy brought the papers to leave them, to see who could get the first one, and then unsolicited all began to read aloud, almost simultaneously, every word in every column. No wonder no one heard anyone else, as everyone, especially the older men, who had nothing to do, but come into town and sit on the street corner, chew, smoke and drink cokes, and usually tell stories that had been heard time and again, but somehow always becoming more embellished as the telling of each of them went along. It had become a source of entertainment. To the younger generation, it was comical. No one believed too much of what any of them had to say, but out of respect, an attentive ear was always loaned, and once again the catch lines became longer, more profound, and once again, another lie told. Oh! Well, they had nothing else to do, and if this meant their existence, then so be it.

Thomas ran to the house, just beyond the Baptist parsonage, stopped, combed his hair, straightened up his shirt, then opened the gate and walked inside the yard. The nice middle aged lady, who appeared much younger than her true age, from her chair, said, "Yes, may I help you?" Thomas placed his hands behind his back, holding them, then cleared his throat, and asked, "I have heard you have a position open here helping someone who is sick?" The lady looked, then replied, "Yes, son, we do, My son who worked in the bank, was shot during an attempted robbery, and he has a very long recuperation time, so we felt it best to hire someone to help take care of him, with the lifting, moving around, and things of this nature. Are you interested in this position?" Thomas replied, "Yes, mam." "Well, then, let's walk inside, and we can discuss this with my son, and see what he thinks." Thomas stood back, allowing Tommy's mother to rise, then turn and walk into the front room of their wood frame home, well built, on the finest street in Greensboro. Entering the room, Thomas saw Tommy, lying in his bed, wrapped in bandages, which seemed to be entwined around him, reading a copy of an old National Geographic, and chewing gum. "Tommy", his mother asked, "we have a young man here, who would like to apply for the job of helping you through your recovery." As Tommy gazed from the book to Thomas, at first he did not realize who it was. When he did, he had a lapse of words, almost not able to speak. His own son had answered the ad to take care of him, making him become both exited and then somewhat restrained.

As Tommy questioned Thomas, making him fully aware of exactly what all was entailed in the job he had applied for; he himself asked Tommy, "well, is this something you would like to try?" With an answer of "Yes, sir", Thomas smiled, realizing that he now was a working man, and he realized he had completely forgotten to ask what the job paid. Turning back, to look, and ask, as he walked out of the room, Tommy, realizing exactly what it was he was doing, looked at him, with a half grin and smirk on his face and said, "ten dollars a week, Sunday's off." Grinning from ear to ear, Thomas walked slowly from the room, then onto the front porch. As he walked down the steps, into the yard, and through the gate, once on the sidewalk, he leapt into the air, clicking his heels, and gave one not so quiet, "yippee". Ten dollars was big money, and now he could really help his mother out. Watching him leave the room, Tommy, watched how he walked, how he held himself, and how he acted. He was a clean cut young man, and he would become someone. Yes, he would succeed.

~ ~ ~

Tommy progressed quicker than the doctor had thought, but still, by no means was he anywhere near being out of the woods. He required much one on one care, having to be helped up and down for bathroom breaks, having someone situate him in the bed to keep from becoming sore, and having someone dress him, at least to the point of being able to receive guests. The job was hard, but Thomas was good, patient, and dedicated. It was as if he had a natural knack for medicine or a medical related work ethic. Tommy embraced the feeling that he now had been given an opportunity to help Thomas. He hoped he could spark an interest in anything that would lead him beyond the back alley café, and the town of Greensboro. Hopes and dreams were wonderful, but the nurturing of his desires was something he felt compelled in doing. After, all Thomas was a product of what had happened between him and Myra many years ago on the banks of Dunn creek. He, then, had no idea, that after all these years, he would be looking into the eyes of something that happened and yet would forever be before him. He had a debt to pay, and if it took him the rest of his life to pay, it would be paid.

Rain poured down onto the roof like cats and dogs. It was a gulley washer, a frog strangler. Would it ever stop? The only consolation was that as it fell onto the tin roof overhang at the back of the house it sounded like a symphony, at least to Tommy anyway. It was music unwritten and played by an orchestra unlike any he had ever heard. Each drop fell; matching distinct notes as only could be imagined in ones mind. As he lay there, the magazine he had been reading slowly faded from his eyesight, falling softly onto the bed. He pulled the blanket closer to his chin, feeling inside warmth that could not be compared to that of an open hearth fire crackling as the logs burned slowly, but rather to the burning desire in his soul to be free of all that troubled him. Lying there, halfway between sleep and awareness, he imagined what it would have been like, had only Myra, a colored girl, been white. Would he have loved her more profoundly? Would he have asked her to attend church socials? Would she have accepted? Would their relationship have blossomed? What if, just what if, had they had grown in love and married? Then, all of this, as it could have been, meant that Thomas would be his son and would have been here with him. What if? He dozed off.

The rain had stopped when Tommy awakened. Surprisingly, there at his bedside, sitting in the rocking chair that had once been his grandmother's sat Myra and beside her, in an old straight backed cane chair, was Thomas. "Well, good afternoon", said Thomas, "how ya doing?" "Fine I guess, just dozed off." "Yes sir, I can see that, you got drool on your chin. Let me wipe that for you, sir", said Thomas. As he leaned over to wipe Tommy's chin, Myra softly said, "Careful son, don't hurt your father." Realizing what she had said, she became embarrassed, and then got up, as if to leave. "No!" exclaimed Tommy, "please sit. I haven't seen you in a while, and I want you to tell me how you are?" The conversation went on for a couple of hours. As the sun began to set, Myra told Tommy that she needed to go, she had things to do, but she would return and visit with him. Tommy reached out for her hand, and as she put her hand in his, he looked at her and said, "Myra, regardless of all the wrong we have done, there is one good and perfect thing that can never be destroyed." As she squeezed his hand, and looked back into his eyes, smiling and with a hint of a tear appearing in her eye she replied, "You are so right. Every time I look at him, I see you, I see what I will never be able to have and experience, and my heart is torn apart each and every time it happens." As she slowly pulled her hand from his, in his eyes, Myra saw tears, making her leaving all the more difficult. She walked from the room, with Thomas, close behind her, speaking to Tommy's mother and father as she stepped onto the front porch. "He's coming around, I pray daily." "Thank you, Myra, thank you so much." She replied. "We pray daily too, and we are so thankful for Thomas and what he means and has meant to Tommy's healing." Myra walked down the sidewalk, her purse hanging from her arm, swaying to and fro, almost like a schoolgirl on her way home from school. She recalled their conversation and thoughts as she walked, each step becoming more and more a bounce, she was feeling cared about, and she, for the first time, in a long time felt like a woman and a lady, without regard to her color. She had finally heard him say, without having heard him exactly, that he did care for her. The look in his eyes had more to say than any words he could have possibly spoken. Still, in the back of her mind, she could not help but think, "Why Lord? Why can't I have what I love so much", then she walked calmly down the street, towards her home.

~ ~ ~

There was still a hint of rain and possibly colder weather still in the air. One of those bone chilling days, when no matter how much you put on for the occasion, it's never enough. Ruts had been formed in the still wet dirt, which now had given way to mucky mud, the kind that is almost like clay, so that when you walk in it, and in Greensboro you couldn't help but walk in it, it was everywhere. You could hear wives and mothers all over yelling, "Wipe off you feet. I been on my knees all day cleaning these floors, now look at them!" Not what you'd call a good day. The promise of better weather, at least clearer weather was in the forecast.

People had stopped talking about the murder on the railroad tracks, life was moving along. But not to worry, there'd be something new any day now, that you could sink your teeth into, and maybe get a good source of gossip. In Greensboro, there was always news, whether it is real news or manufactured news, but we had news. With gasoline costing fifteen cents a gallon, surely people would need to start walking more. How could they survive paying those exorbitant prices? People were lined up daily at the welfare office, picking up their commodities, a government subsidy program. It wasn't really that bad. The peanut butter, grape jelly, and crackers, made a meal all by itself. Of course, depending on how many there were in your family dictated how much you were allowed to get. There were people who needed commodities, but refused to accept them. They would rather do without than sponge off the government. After all, it was a democratic give away, or so they said. To others, it was a way of reaping the benefits of what taxes they may have paid over time, and now it was their turn to collect on their endeavors. Regardless, it saved a lot of people, especially during this time. You could get cornmeal, flour, sugar, cheese, grape jelly, peanut butter, powdered eggs, and from time to time even hard rock candy, for which all the children thought Christmas had arrived early.

Families in Greensboro, with exception of those who lived in town, worked hard on their farms. Little time was spent leaving the farm to come to town, so when they did everyone usually made a day of it, or if there were relatives living there, some would come, spend the day, get supplies, spend the night with relatives, then return the next day. For children, this was a treat. It meant an opportunity to visit the East End, a restaurant, set up in an old railroad diner, with a building addition onto it, located just to the East of town on old highway twenty-eight. They had booths, a soda fountain and bar, and they served both cooked meals and fast food meals. The jukebox was always playing, each selection chosen costing five cents. Teenagers even danced there. Later as time went on it became a hangout for "hoods", the unruly teenage crowd who generally wore tee shirts, with the sleeves rolled up and packages of cigarettes rolled in them. The style of the day was long hair, slicked back with enough oil that if you were determined to, you could grease your universal with it, and it had to be combed with a wave included in it. The girls wore short skirts, bobby socks and usually had ribbons or pigtails in their hair.

"Good morning Tommy", said Myra as she entered his room. "Hi, how are you this morning", said Tommy. "I'm fine, and am happy that you are. Thomas will be late today. He had another chore to do, so to keep you from struggling on your own, I decided that I would come and stay, if it's okay with you?" "Sure", said Tommy, as he pulled himself back into his bed, bringing himself into a sitting position. "Well, Myra, I guess I made a fool out of myself the other day….I apologize if it embarrassed you." "Oh! Tommy, hush, now, you know better than that. We have known each other for many years, and there is nothing you could say that would embarrass or hurt me, because I just know that it's not in your nature." "I appreciate your confidence, Myra", said Tommy, "but, I just want you to know that I meant it when I told you I have thought about you all through the years……I mean it." She sat at the foot of his bed, and looked at him. "Tommy, you are white and I am colored, and you know, as much as you or I might wish to be beyond that, in Mississippi it just is not going to happen and I have accepted that, and I will live with it." Tommy replied, "but Myra, surely you wanted to marry, or will marry, I mean." "Tommy," replied Myra, "my heart, for most of my life, has belonged to only one person, and if it means that I can have nothing more than association with that person, then I accept it. Neither you nor I can change anything; we can only live with it. I had hoped early on things would change, but they didn't, and neither you nor I can do anything now to make it any other way. But, I can tell you this, and I tell you this in confidence, and honesty. I do not want anyone else. God never promised me a white man or a colored man, but it was you I found,

Where Cotton Grows

and it was you who found me. Yes, we have a son, a son we cannot walk down the street together with, because of who we are, and what we are. Truthfully, I do not want my son to live that kind of life. I want him to go far away where he can be judged on what he knows, and how he conducts himself. He has a lot of you in him, and I am reminded of that every time I look at him. He walks like you, holds his head like you, pops his knuckles on his hands like you, and his mannerisms are almost identical. I see you every minute of every day, so I am never far away from you. I kiss you each night before I lie down, because each time I see Thomas, and each time I kiss him goodnight, I see you. So, without you, I think not. I am with you even when you don't know I am I have Thomas". Tommy reached for her hand and she extended hers to him. As he spoke, his voice choked back a quiver in his voice. In a soft voice, as he rubbed the back of her hand with his index finger of his right hand, he said, "Myra, I have had the opportunity to marry, almost did. I got cold feet. I didn't get cold feet because of being afraid to say "I do", I got cold feet because I didn't have the heart to walk away from you. I felt like a traitor. I know we couldn't marry, and do you know how that makes me feel? I feel like I have eternally made you live the life of a harlot. To me, that has eaten away at my soul ten times harder than all the rest of it. I know you for who you are. You are a descent woman, a good mother, and without any reservations you would be a wonderful wife. I have never seen your color, but I have seen your eyes, as they lit up like moonbeams when you walked home in the dark. I have seen the radiance of your smile and I have felt its warmth, and yes, I have felt your touch and the inner strength I was given by it. You are a lady, and I am separated from you only by bias and hate. It's not right, and I have done you wrong for so long. I can never beg for your forgiveness enough. I am far beneath you in dignity, for it is you who have endured the pain and suffering, not I. You are the one who had the baby, you are the one who paid the price, and you still protected me, while I did nothing to protect you. I knew you loved me, and in my heart, I have always loved you, but I was afraid, and just a boy. I should have done the right thing, the honorable thing, but I didn't, and now I have to live with it and I have to die with it. I pray that before I die, you can find it in your heart to forgive me. Thomas is a beautiful boy. I am so proud of him, and yet I cannot even acknowledge him in public, my own son! My father, as far as I know has never known he is a grandfather, and to tell him now would kill him, as bad as I hate to say it. Please, Myra, please forgive me?" She kissed his softly on the lips as she leaned over to pull the sheet up to him, and whispered in his ear, "Tommy, in my heart, you are the only man, and I now know how you feel about me. I can die, if the Lord sees fit to call me, and be happy with his decision." She smiled, touched his face with her hand, turned and left the room. She had to go home and feed Thomas lunch.

Little had changed with exception to weather and the few that had died in recent months and years. Even the cracks in the sidewalks continued to grow while grass in places pushed itself up and through clinging to every ounce of life it could muster. The flowers bloomed, trees blossomed, and old men still sat on coca-cola cases in the filling stations, chewed tobacco, placed checkers on a homemade checkerboard, using coca cola bottle caps as the pieces. Of course, they still spit their tobacco juice in the old wood burning stove near where they sat. Stories still found their way into every conversation no matter how many times they had been told. Many through the years had even taken on a new blend of mix in telling them, but if you listened carefully you could remember them. Some things never change, but that's a good thing.

~ ~ ~

Arthritis and rheumatism had become constant partners in the life of Miss Jean, Miss Nellie and the older citizenship of Greensboro, making their ability to come and go with less ease as they once enjoyed. In their vocabulary it was often referred to as maturity, but we knew it as old age. Miss Jean still went to work, she still could be found on weekends in her yard digging in the dirt, after a trip to the old home place. She never made a trip without obtaining several cuttings of plants that she often would find as she passed a heavy thicket, and in a glimpse might catch a lonely redbud or wild hydrangea just setting there waiting to be unearthed and brought back to her yard for tender loving card. Her yard was a wildflower haven, even the birds found safe haven there. She would often refer to her garden as a bird sanctuary. She took so much pleasure in just sitting and watching wildlife enjoy the freedom to come into her yard and feel enough freedom to walk up to a feeder and replenish themselves. She'd always laugh and say, "Look at that rascal." She was a friend to all. In secrecy she was an avid painter, and had many paintings to her credit painted on china that was displayed generously throughout her home. She never took credit for anything, but gave credit to everyone. In the fall her living room was like a dried leaf storage unit. She would go around to all the yards in Greensboro selecting colorful leaves that were still on trees, and breaking or cutting off the branches, would bring them home and lay them throughout her home for them to dry. She made flower arrangements that were regularly used in the church and although she never took credit for this, she loved doing it.

A young boy came running down the street, face as red as a beet, barely able to catch his breath, with eyes just as big as saucers, and eyelashes batting ninety to nothing. "Granny, Granny", yelled the young man, "Woolworth's is about to have the drawin!" That drawing meant ten dollars, cold cash, and enough groceries to provide nearly a month's worth of meals, so yes, it was big doings, The lady quickly grabbed her purse, and lit a shuck down the street, and for a woman of stout stature, may I say once she got to rolling, there was no need for airbrakes, she needed a barricade! Rumors around town had it that when she backed up, she beeped! On one occasion, a friend of hers made the statement, thinking she wasn't around, but later learned that she was, that if she had to run for her life and haul tail, it most assuredly would be a two trip job. But, she took the ribbing all in good spirit, just as long as she was able to stand there in the blazing heat waiting for the Woolworth's Manager to come out with the big bullhorn to call out the lucky numbers. Cranes were standing by, just in case she won, and accidentally passed out or fell down. No, not really, but they did keep an eye on her.

∽ ∽ ∽

When Thomas neared his final year of school, Myra, with Tommy's help, began to discuss where Thomas would attend college. Tommy had offered to handle his education, and agreed to send him to any school he chose to attend, provided he made the grade and kept his academic standing up. Of course, with this promise, Thomas would have agreed to real estate on the moon, but realistically, and by now, he knew that Tommy was his dad, and that Tommy had for quite a while now been giving Myra money to see that he had the things he needed. Thomas in time had grown to respect Tommy, and although he found it strange that this white man was his father, he had begun to feel the overwhelming urge, to call him, "Dad". Of course, as of yet, he had never dared do it, but he had sure given it much thought. Over and over, as Thomas tried to rationalize this entire situation, he could not help but wonder, "Why, am I as I am? What have I done, that would have ever caused me to be disliked by God, or made to endure and live as I have lived since birth." Such as this was hard for an adult to understand, not to mention a young man, but though he thought this, he never verbalized it and he never would. He loved his mother and he respected Tommy, actually he loved Tommy, because he knew who he was, but he wasn't sure if he was quite ready to go there with the love part right yet. He'd think on this, kind of let it lie for a while, then revisit the subject matter, and go from there. He was open to it, but not just now.

On Thomas' eighteenth birthday, another letter arrived unexpectedly in the mail, and addressed to him at the residence of his grandparents, where he and his mother lived, and always had lived. It lay on the table, no one recognizing it. Thomas' grandfather had gone to get the mail, this was included, and he just laid everything on the table as he always did. Upon arrival, Thomas, as he always did, checked the mail, and there it was, a letter addressed to him, and the writing looked familiar. As he opened the letter, you could hear him say, "Uh oh, it's another one of them anonymous letters with money in it for me. Thomas had received one of these letters every year for as long as he could recall, and each year, maybe not written exactly the same word for word, but surely with the same intended content, it always let him know that angels were watching over him, and he was being watched, and once he would turn the note over, there folded neatly he always found a crisp one hundred dollar bill, brand new, and smelling of fresh ink. Myra, against Thomas' counter, had always made him set the money aside. She wanted her son to have a good start in life, it meant a lot to her to be able to say that her son was not going to have to scrap and labor as had she. His life would be better; not easier, but surely better, and he would be educated. This she vowed! As before, all the other times, Thomas again picked up the letter, opened it, and there the same noted basically, and once again the crisp one hundred dollar bill. Except, this time there was another note that had been paper clipped to the note which had been written. When he opened this note, it said, "Please, at your convenience, but not later than this specified date, stop by the office of Killebrew Law Office." Thomas got real quiet then, what had he done?

The next day could not have arrived any sooner, as Thomas was up before dawn, dressed, with note in hand, and as soon at eight o'clock in the morning arrived, he would be at the door of Killebrew Law Office to see exactly what this was all about. He knew he was not guilty of anything, but what was this all about? As he sat there on the stoop, he counted the minutes almost one by one, growing more and more impatient. Finally, a car pulled up in front and out stepped Mr. Killebrew, who always came in to the office early. Thomas stood up, nodded his head, and introduced himself to Mr. Killebrew. "Ah, yes", said Mr. Killebrew, "please, come on in, I can make an exception this time. Please come into my office and sit while I start the coffee." Thomas thanked him, took a seat, still nervous, but knowing he had done nothing, so it was now a matter of waiting to see what the outcome was. As Mr. Killebrew came back, he entered the office, peered from over his glasses as they slid slightly down his nose, then walked around to his chair, pulled it back, turned it, and sat down. Mr. Killebrew said, "Son, do you believe in angels?" "What kind of a question was this, and especially coming from a lawyer, one who had the ability to squeeze blood from a turnip, with absolutely no remorse? Did he believe in angels?? Well, yes, he did, but what business was it of his? As Mr. Killebrew, waited, Thomas, raised his head, and with a sheepish look replied, "Yes, Yes sir, I do." "Good", said Mr. Killebrew, "because, son, there has been an angel watching you since the day you were being held in your mother's arms while she was walking home, but you wouldn't remember that, would you? Lawyer Killebrew chuckled. "I don't think so", said Thomas. "Well, son," said lawyer Killebrew, "in my profession, rarely do I get paid to be a messenger of good will, but in this case, someone very special has tasked me with delivering some very good news to you. Well, would you like to hear what the good news is?" "Yes, sir, I would", said Thomas. "Okay son, just listen, I will read you something, Once I finish, if you need clarification, I will re-read, and then I will answer your questions, okay?" Asked lawyer Killebrew? Lawyer Killebrew then began to read. It was a letter, but who wrote it? It read: Thomas, I will never forget the first time I saw you, just a baby, wrapped in a blanket, snug in your mother's arms, and out in the rain, but she was doing her best to get you home and out of the rain. Thomas, I know you and you should not be ashamed of who you are for any reason. I know your mother and I know your father. My heart aches for you, because she has never been able to know the real presence and love of a father, and he, your father being so near. I know the love of a child, and I love you. I saw in you, and I will never forget, in the rain that day, it was almost as if a little halo was over your head, and to me it was like an omen, one I could not turn away from, So I stopped, gave you and your mother a ride, and from that moment until now, I have always kept and eye on you, Oh! I have seen you from afar, but I have always been there, watching and listening patiently. Thomas, I want to help you. It is my duty, I feel it. Be cautious with my gift. Be frugal, thrifty and use it wisely and sparingly. Remember, I am watching you. I have decided to set up a trust in your name, of which you will be allowed to use the interest to fund your education, and at a date and time to be determined, I will, in conclusion and upon my demise, bequeath to you everything in its entirety. This is a gift I love you. You were such a beautiful little baby boy, so poor, and so alone in this world. I had to keep an eye on you. Do not dwell on who I am, it is not important; rather what is more important is what you do with this gift. Be sweet and happy birthday, Thomas, with Love. That's all it said, no name? Who did this? As Thomas sat there the Lawyer smiled and said, "See, there are angels, and you have your own personal one!" Excited, Thomas ran home, all the way, he could not wait to tell Myra, and for that matter, Tommy too. He would have to wait to tell Tommy when he went to work, later on in the morning, but he would tell him.

~ ~ ~

As Thomas boarded the bus, he turned to his mother and said, "Well, this is it, finally going to college, I'll miss you." With tears in her eyes, Myra hugged and kissed him on the cheek and lips, ran her hand over his head, and straightened his shirt and tie. Thomas was leaving, and Myra's life would have a void. It scared her, what would she do? The bus, rolled off into the day, East on Highway 28, making it's way through small farming communities, where cattle were grazing in pastures, horses were slowly walking from one feeding spot to another, then around bends and curves. He watched anxiously as he passed places he had neither seen nor knew existed. A new world lay before him, one of excitement, enchantment and opportunity, and he realized this. For a fleeting moment, a tear came to his eye. Behind him was everything he had ever know and cared about. Greensboro had been the only place he had ever known. He already missed the smell of hamburgers cooking on the large grill, the sizzle of the ground beef as it was laid on the griddle to cook, the smell of the onions as they heated, releasing the tantalizing aromas into the kitchen, spreading throughout the café. What would he do? How would he survive this separation? His mind then turned to his goals, his aim and his opportunity to become educated. He had dreams; he would reach heights of intellectual notoriety. He would make his mother proud, and he would come home to Greensboro and settle. He wanted to see his mother live a life of comfort and ease. No longer would she have to stand and work, no longer would she wait tables, clean kitchens and be dependent on the alms of those whom she served. No, sir! She would be a stay-at-home-lady, secure in the surroundings of the home he would provide for her.

∼ ∼ ∼

The line was overwhelming; he had never seen so many people, especially colored people, and all in one place, here for the same

Mike Reed

reason. As he reached the head of the line, he gave the papers he had brought with him; he was assigned a room, given a schedule of orientation, and shown where the facilities and dining hall was. As he passed the dining hall he couldn't help but notice that there were no smells of good home cooked food coming from it. All he smelled was what he thought might have been the smell of coffee, and several people sitting, wearing white uniforms, smoking cigarettes, and laughing. This was it, this is where he would eat, and try to survive. He had his doubts. A voice came from behind him, "Good morning, already hungry?" When he turned to acknowledge who had asked the question, his eyes became large, and he found difficulty in speaking. It was Marcel, the girl who worked in the office. As Marcel, grinned, Thomas lowered his head, and said, "No, not hungry, and from the smell of things in there, I won't be anytime soon." Marcel, placing her hand on the sleeve of his coat said, "Well, it's not your mama's cooking, but in two to three days, you'll be happy to get it. When you finish finding everything, and if you have time, stop by the office, and I'll brief you on some other things you will need to know." "Okay", said Thomas, "I'll be there." They smiled, and she turned and walked away, he watching her as she made her way down the long corridor and up the stairs, turning into the main hall that led to the Office of the Dean and where she worked.

Knocking on the door, and hearing a soft, "come in", Thomas entered the office where Marcel worked. She smiled, and arose from her seat, walking to the counter that separated him from the inner part of her office. Marcel exclaimed, "Well, I see you found me. Let's see if we can get you all straightened out, and on a safe course here." Smiling, Thomas replied, "Well, I'm here, but as to how safe the course is, only time will tell." She went over his schedule, explaining each class, where they met, the times, when he needed to be up and present for breakfast, lunch and supper, then lights out, and the curfew. It was all new to him, but he was okay.

Thomas was beginning to feel like he was an inmate. He'd never experienced such as this before. The extent of his accountability had normally been limited to his mother's instructions. He was now in another world, but from where he stood, and the scope of his visibility, it was a world that he surely did not mind being in. From where he stood, what he saw looked pretty good, and he didn't mind taking a few more minutes of the view in. Marcel just stood there smiling at him. Thomas, realizing all of sudden that he was caught, became a little embarrassed, and then saying, "Sorry didn't mean to stare", turned and left her office. Shaking her head, and with a woman's little grin, she went back to her seat and started her work.

～ ～ ～

Myra felt like a mama cow whose calf had just been weaned. She found herself calling for him, and then realizing he wasn't there, she would take her apron and wipe her eyes. He really wasn't that far away, but she couldn't walk to him, and it hurt her. He was alone, on his own, and mama couldn't guide him.

As Myra walked to Tommy's house, she entered finding him sitting in a chair by the table, writing. "Good morning", "Good morning Myra, how are ya?" "Tommy, I am as lost as I can be", "He's gone, I can't see him, and I miss him." Tommy reached and touched her hand and said, "Myra, I miss him too, but he's grown now, and this is what young men do. You need to let him go, and let him make his way. You have taught him well, he's a good boy, and he will do the right thing. This I know for a fact", and while saying this Tommy looking at Myra, winked and smiled. She moved closer to him, putting her hand on his shoulder, leaning over she said, "Yes, he is a good boy. He's just a chip off the old block." The two laughed, he dropped his head snickering. "What's for breakfast this morning?" "Are you hungry?" "Yes, I am", said Tommy, "I believe I'll have a big piece of humble pie." Both laughed and she went to the kitchen to cook his breakfast. As Tommy, with the help of a walking stick, made his way to the table, Myra pulled back the chair for him. He looked at her, then asking, "Where's your plate?" Myra, smiling, said "You want me to sit and eat with you?" "It's a special day Myra. Our son has gone away to college, and for the first time, I can see where he gets his personality, charm and good looks." Myra blushed, "Tommy, be careful, I don't want you to get into trouble." "Trouble", said Tommy, this is my house, and you are here with me, and if I ask you to sit and eat, then you have that right, so sit?" Then sheepishly he added a "Please", looking up to her like a little boy, reminding her of how he had looked when she first met him on the banks of Dunn Creek. She smiled, picked up her plate from the stove, walked over placed it on the table, set her cup of coffee down, then took her seat. As Tommy looked across the table at her, he reminded her of how beautiful she was, how she still had the look of a little girl, and how her eyes brightened up the room. He commented on her hair, and how perfect she was, then held out his hand, and taking hers in his, looked into those eyes, and said, "Thank you so much for such a wonderful son, and for all the sacrifices you made, for both he and me." "Myra, I have never said this, but you must have known all along, I love you, and I have always loved you, not being able to have what you want most in your life has humbled me beyond anything I can tell you. I am so proud of you." Myra cried, got up from her chair, walked around the table and kissed Tommy. "I love you, too, and like I told you before, I will always have you, because I have Thomas." He wiped her tears, held her close, patted her back, and they finished their breakfast.

Tommy, nearing full recuperation, had begun to make plans to return to work. The doctor, pleased with his healing, had advised a slow progression back into his work schedule. For Tommy, it was freedom; he could resume a normal life. Myra's fear was that it would again separate her from what she had grown to feel comfortable with, and now it was being pulled from beneath her feet. She could show no signs of discontentment, she wanted Tommy well and healthy, but she did not want to give him up again, even if it meant no more cooking, cleaning and nursing him. She sank into minor depression, forgetting about things she had once lived to do. No longer, so she thought, would she walk the street to Tommy's, and no longer be able to see him and talk to him. "Myra, you have outdone yourself on this roast", Tommy praised. "The whole meal is beyond consumption, I would prefer to just sit and look at it, and you have really outdone yourself." Thanking him, she placed her fork back on her plate, and took her dishes to the sink. Tommy, watching her noticed she had a look of despair on her face. "Myra, what is it? Have I said something to offend you?" "No", replying Myra, "I have realized that with you returning to work, you will no longer need me to come and do for you, and it's not the money, it's the not having anyone." Tommy, looking at her, had realized she felt alone again, she had no one. "Myra, I still will have a need here in the house, what makes you think this? I never said anything about discontinuing your services here." She turned and looked, "Do you mean you still want me to come and work here?" "Yes and why not? Housework is never ending, and no one does it the way you do, and to be truthful, I've grown accustomed having you around. So if you agree, I would very much like to have you come here regularly and cook for me, and take care of the house." Her eyes brightened, she hummed softly, then turned and began to wash the dishes.

~ ~ ~

"I got a letter from Thomas today." "You did?" replied Tommy, "how is he? How's he doing? "He's studying hard, making good grades?" "Yes he is, and he says to tell you hello." Tommy leaned back in his chair rubbed his chin, then asked Myra, "Would like to drive up one afternoon late, and pay him a surprise visit?" "What, you mean? Actually get in a car, and drive all that way?" "Yes, why not, the roads are paved, the car has gas, and my work schedule is only half a day, so why not?" It was settled, and they laughed, sharing thoughts about Thomas. Of course, they had no idea how it would affect Thomas, but none the less, it was settled, and they would go. Myra, had cleaned the kitchen, finished everything and by noon they were in the car, driving East on Highway 28, making their way to see Thomas. Passing fields of picked-over cotton they drove along at a speedy rate of fifty miles per hour, enjoying the sights, talking like school kids, enjoying each others company, and of course, discussing their son. When it was just the two of them, they felt the freedom to discuss their life, as they had come to know it, realizing it would never be more than what they now had. They chose not to dwell on the what-if, rather to put their thoughts to good use, making sure their interest and concerns were given to Thomas.

Where Cotton Grows

As the car turned into the main entrance of the campus, Myra, placing her hand on her chest, gasped and said, "What if he doesn't want to see us? "What if he doesn't want to see us? Woman, how can you make a statement like that? He's his mama's boy, and I can't think of ever recalling when he didn't want to see you, can you?" Regardless, Myra had reservations; this was all new to her. She had seldom traveled any distance from Greensboro, and this was another world, with big buildings, all red brick, and large oak trees, benches everywhere, with students sitting and reading, some talking and laughing. Yes, it was all Greek to her.

As they exited the car, Tommy told Myra to come with him to the Dean's office. They climbed the steps walking into the large foyer, then right into the Dean's office. Entering, they were met by Marcel, who asked, "How may I help you?" Tommy spoke up saying, "We'd like to see Thomas ...." Before Tommy could get Thomas' last name out, Marcel lit up like a beacon, saying, "Wait right here sir." How strange, he hadn't even given her his last name, and already she had left in search of him. Returning, Marcel smiled, and said, "Yes, Thomas is in class, but within the next half hour, he should be coming along that walkway right there in front, on his way to his next class. Would you like for me to leave a message, and let him know you're here?" Tommy replied, "No, we'll just sit there on the bench and when we see him, we'll talk a little."

They waited for what seemed to be an eternity, and then as the student body began to dwindle out of the buildings changing classes, they looked eagerly for the first glimpse of what they had grown to miss so much. All of a sudden Myra stood up, looking towards the door of the science lab. There coming out the door, she saw the tall frame of a young man, no longer resembling that of a little boy. She put both hands over her mouth, and tears welled up in her eyes, and not thinking, reached and grabbed Tommy by the hand saying, "There he is, Tommy, our son!" It scared her, she had voiced her feelings, and turning to Tommy she apologized for having said it. Tommy, as quick as she had said it, turned to Myra and said, "Yes, and may I say he is a fine looking young man, Looks a lot like me.", smiled at Myra, and grabbed her hand, the Myra, slowed released the grip. She called for Thomas, as he noticed them, he ran to them, hugging Myra, and saying, "Mama, what are you doing here?" Then Myra, looking elated and overcome with emotion, before she thought said, "Your father and I wanted to see you, baby." Thomas, standing there startled by what she had said, gave way to a smile, and said, "It's good to see you and dad." Tommy had never heard the word before, especially being said to him, but it was true, and he didn't mind. Thomas was his son, good, bad, or indifferent. What was done was done, and this was the real McCoy. He felt no shame, rather he beamed with pride. His son was in college, and being half-colored and half-white at the moment didn't bother him. Thomas was his and his with Myra. How he had wished, this could have been under other circumstances.

He had finally realized he was now is a situation that would never change, and would never be able to go beyond this. He felt both a success and a failure. What had he done? He didn't think. He had ruined the lives of three people, and had placed them in a status that would affect them until the day each died. How could he have possibly been so stupid? And he loved Myra, and he loved Thomas, his family, his life, and in Mississippi. He could never publicly brag, he could never accept ownership, he could never allow himself to go beyond where he now was. It was a mess, but one filled with love. He ached for the world he had created for Thomas. It would not change, and if word ever got out, it would certainly mean trouble. He had nowhere to go, no one to confide in, and no way out. They were all sealed in a nucleus of here and now.

The trip home was a quite one. Tommy had sunk to an all time low. Not because of Myra or Thomas, but of the knowing it would never be, never change, and never get any better than now. It was a dead end road.

～ ～ ～

A mockingbird chirped in the tree just outside the window and she turned to see if she could see it, Myra laid her Bible aside on the table, leaned forward and looked with intent surveillance. It was there, she could hear it, but its illusive intent escaped her sight. She waited patiently, listening to the sound it made. No worries, just a peace engulfed her. Truly, this was the place, one of solitude and contentment. Her eyes began to close, as she sat there between half sleep and awareness. She thought of Thomas and of Tommy. Her world, though she had no real connection other than brief meetings throughout time, was one of separation. She thought of her son away in college, of what he might be doing and how he had grown and matured. She sank into a peaceful world of silence.

There was a knock at he door; it was the mailman. Would there be a letter from Thomas, or could it be just circulars and the weekly newspaper? She felt sad; there had been no letter in a week. Surely he had time to write, but then maybe he was studying for a test, who knew? At any rate, she was forever thinking of him-what he was doing, was he well, did he eat enough, and did he have his clothes laundered regularly? A mother never stops worrying, certainly not her. Thomas was her world, and to give him up, to share him with the wonder and excitement of college, was almost more than she could bare, but in her heart, she sacrificed yet again, because she knew she was doing the right thing.

A horn honked, she got up to go see who it could be. Arriving at the door, she looked through the screen to see Tommy coming up the walkway to the front porch. As she opened the door she invited him in and asked him to have a seat. Was this a business visit or a pleasure call? Tommy looked at Myra and said, "I have to go to Memphis tomorrow, bank business. I wished you could go. We could stop by the school and visit Thomas." Myra, with a far-off look in her eyes said, "How long will you be gone?" "At the most, it will be maybe a day or two. Is there something I can do for you or get for you while I'm there?" "Thank you, but no, I have more than enough to keep me busy here, I'll be all right, you just remember to drive careful." As he left, Tommy had a weakened feeling, like someone had knocked the very wind out of him. Getting into the car, he turned and glanced, smiled, then closed the door and drove off. Myra stood on the stoop until the car turned and drove back onto the street. Even though she knew better, she felt an absence when he drove from sight.

She was standing in the kitchen, ironing, when her elderly father came through the door. He never had much to say, just an occasional grunt, walking to the ice box to get some cold tea, or maybe a snack. This time he just stood there, with a blank and gaping stare on his face. "Myra, I have some news, you ought to sit down." Her heart

Where Cotton Grows

sank, was it Thomas? Was he sick, had he been hurt, what was wrong? "Myra, its Tommy" He told her. Fear sprang through her as if she had been hit with one thousand volts of electricity. "Tommy? What about Tommy?" asked Myra? "Honey, there was a wreck last night, near Silas, on the worst part of the road…it was Tommy." "Papa is he all right?" asked Myra. "Honey, I know everything you know, and I know what went on between you two, but Tommy is dead." Myra ran from the kitchen into her room, slammed the door, and with her hand held over her mouth. "NO!" The screams came from her room. Sobbing so loud, inconsolable, her father opened the door and walked into the room. "Myra, grieving is good, but he's better off…..it was a bad wreck, from what I heard, the car is not even recognizable. He hit a tree then rolled down an embankment and into a creek. The car burned." She laid there on the bed, face in the pillow, sobbing as she never had before. This was the end for her; no more would she feel a whole woman. Though never married to him, she considered Tommy her husband, and in his heart she knew she was his wife. They never lived together, but their hearts were never apart. Now she had the unwanted job of telling Thomas his father was dead. Though Thomas had never lived with his father, or known him wholly as a father, Tommy was still his daddy, and he did feel a connection. Not today, not tomorrow, not ever.

∼ ∼ ∼

Miss Jean had heard the news. She was on her way home from the office, driving by the road leading to where Myra lived. She drove up, parked, turned off the ignition, opened her door, and walked up to the porch. As she stepped onto the porch, Myra's father met her at the door, saying, "Miss Jean, how can I help you?" "May I see Myra? I just have to talk to her." Miss Jean, walking into Myra's room, found her lying on the bed, faces into her pillow and sobbing loudly. Walking up to her and placing her aging hand on Myra's back, rubbing it, she said, "Honey, can I take you someplace, or get something for you? I heard at the office, honey, I am so sorry, believe me. I am so sorry." She reached down and pulled Myra to her, holding her tightly in her arms, rocking back and forth. "It'll be okay, I promise, you have a lot to live for, and life has not forgotten about you." Miss Jean spent much of the afternoon with Myra, consoling her, was trying to cheer her up. "We'll get through this honey, tomorrow will be better."

Tommy was buried in Greensboro cemetery on a sunny afternoon in the shade of the largest oak tree in the cemetery. How befitting a resting place for one who loved the shade of trees and the symbol of the old south. Myra attended, stood in the background, cried with everyone, and remembered her Tommy as she would always remember him, a tall lanky boy, with a big smile, long hair and combed neatly. She glanced over at Thomas, crying too, and in him seeing once again, the very image of Tommy. Placing her hand in Thomas', she smiled and closed her eyes, for now, in her heart, she was publicly holding the hand of the boy she had always loved, and she was doing it in public, without anyone having anything to say about it. She could do it for as long as she liked and whenever she liked. He was finally all hers. He lived in her heart, and in the very soul of her son.

One by one, the funeral party descended the cemetery hill, but Myra held back, waiting for all to leave. When just she and Thomas were left standing there all alone beside the grave, she reached into her blouse, pulled out a tiny cross, and with her hands began to dig a small hole in the fresh shoveled dirt. Placing the cross, wrapped up in a napkin, in the hole she had dug, then covering it with dirt, she murmured a silent prayer, and tearfully clutched her chest, and said "Good bye, Tommy, and thank you." She walked slowly down the path to the road where they wailed back home.

The walk, a good three quarters of a mile, gave them both time to reflect and remember just what Tommy's life had meant to them. Thomas reflected on how Tommy always took the time to talk to him, and show him kindness, how he had always invented little jobs for him to do, they seemingly had paid him far more than it was worth. Neither ashamed of their secret, they walked on. Myra held her son's hand, never letting it go, and smiled the entire time. Thomas was unsure what caused her to smile, but suspected that it was best he didn't ask. Some things are better left alone, and he was sure this was one of those times to say nothing, and just walk, letting her clutch his hand.

∽ ∽ ∽

Thomas returned to school, and Myra continued on with her job, seeming to work longer, harder and more often than she ever had before. It was said that she was consumed with Tommy's death, she went for days without eating, and she would buy things, and walk out without taking them with her. Several began to talk, but no one was sure of exactly what was the matter. Many in town had known about the birth of her illegitimate baby, and many suspected who the father was, but at that time, several had been accused of being the father, so no one really ever knew for sure, except Miss Jean and a few others, and Miss Jean never talked. It was not of her nature, and she did not gossip, and detested those who did.

In time Myra seemed to overcome her depression, she continued to work in the café, and since Tommy's death had not continued in her housekeeping employment. She just didn't have it in her. It seemed she learned to tolerate life, but was never completely at peace with anything except Thomas and his ambitions. Thomas was now in his second year at school and doing very well. His grades were good and he was stellar student. He had excelled in mathematics and science and had expressed a interest in the field of medicine to his mother. Myra was proud, and encouraged him. He was all she had now, he was her life.

Her days were consumed by growing flowers, working in the yard, and doing whatever she could to keep her mind off other things. With Thomas being away, she had reverted to where she had been when she first met Tommy, just a girl, living at home with her parents, and with no future. In Thomas she sensed a future, but not wanting to make him feel obligated, she never brought the subject up. Of course, Thomas, in every conversation they had always included his mama as living with him, and her being the mistress of the house, but Myra knew, that in time to pass this would change, but deep inside she prayed it wouldn't.

Myra's roses were the prettiest in town. She had crawled every inch of the yard on her hands and knees, and had babied them as if they were children. She talked to them as she worked with them, she touched them with love, and it seemed as though they responded to her. She was pleased with her ability to nurture her plants; they gave her a deep sense of satisfaction and accomplishment. Everyone in town, at one time or another, would come by and look at her flower garden; it was really something to see.

Later that year, Myra's father passed away. He was buried in the colored cemetery just beyond and joining the white cemetery on cemetery hill. Separated only by a fence, both graveyards were side by side, and almost one. Myra had buried him near her mother, who had died a short time prior. She was now alone, in a world she knew little about, other that life on the alley where the café was, and where she lived. She resolved to continue on in her flower garden, and fix up her home as best she could, though in some ways it had already begun to show signs of rotten wood squeaks and creaks in the floors, and in the colder season it seemed more difficult to keep it as warm as it once was. Everything in her world was growing old even her. She still had her dreams, she had her memories, and she still had Thomas. She was blessed, she was thankful, and yes, she had truthfully had the best of both worlds, still having a living part it.

The democrats were re-elected. What did it mean for her? She had heard word of voting rights, but she had no concept of this, as she had never voted. Many of the churches were having rallies, held in secret, so as not to stir up the Ku Klux Klan, but how could you keep something like this a secret. It was freedom, it was liberty, and it's something she had always dreamed of. She thought to herself, that it was too late. Equal rights for her no longer held the meaning that it once did. What if she could have dated Tommy, without having to slip around and do it? What if they had really gotten married? Though in her heart it never really mattered, she had always considered him her husband. He was all she had ever wanted and now he was gone. The Lord knew her love for him, and what was in her heart. She would not apologize for loving him. Love knew no color, no boundary. Besides love was of the heart, something deep down inside you.

~ ~ ~

People came and solicited signatures to support the colored right to vote. Myra was afraid to sign, for fear of reprisal. She was not a trouble-starter, not someone to cause problems. She liked her world quiet and peaceful. Marches had already begun to happen in places such as the capitol and more speakers representing the colored movement had arrived and started working in Greensboro. It was not a comfortable time. It meant only trouble. For a good cause sure, but bloodshed was sure to follow. It always did. She could not separate herself from who she was, and the things in her life, but thinking of Thomas, she felt compelled to at least do what she could to try and bring about a peaceful solution. Peace, as prayed for during this time, was rare. The white felt infringed upon, felt like they were being forced to do what they felt they never should do. White still regarded colored as niggers, and recalling the reason how they had happened here in the first place just did not make it easier. It was a time of turmoil, and the road ahead would promise to be bumpy. Myra attended the rallies in the local churches she sat attentively, listened to all the dreams, heard the promises, was led to believe the vote was just around the corner, then asked once again to sacrifice for a worthy cause. She joined the movement, and became a card carrier. To her, this was mostly all formality, for she had no intention of being consumed by anything more than Thomas.

Thomas had told his mother that he had joined the movement, and had become an active participant, which scared Myra to death. She could not bear to think of him beaten up, bleeding, and possibly killed. These were the realities of such a movement. The speakers, those who instigated these events, would organize, and then inspire the locals to participate, and it was the locals who usually took the brunt of the aggression. Myra did not want this for Thomas. She would write him and she would tell him face to face. A rally was organized in Greensboro, to be held at the court house in Gore city first, and then they would walk to Greensboro, and through town. It was to be a peaceful rally that is until the Ku Klux Klan showed up. Greensboro had an active Klan following, but few knew exactly who they were. It was rumored who was and was not inclusive in the membership, but no proof existed. Myra didn't care, just as long as she was left out of it. She wanted no part of trouble, and this spelled trouble.

～ ～ ～

Sitting on a bench and dressed in her Sunday best Myra waited for Thomas at the bus station. He was coming home for a visit, and she was on cloud nine. It had been months since she had enjoyed the pleasure of watching him sit and eat, drink tea by the pitcher full, and nap on the couch, as she sat quietly observing his every breath. She noticed his facial Hair. He had started shaving, and his hands, how masculine and nicely formed they were. She sat in such amazement, of how something so perfect had been conceived and formed inside of her. She was a very observant mother, and one who guarded and protected her young. She couldn't fight back the tears, for each time she noticed things about him she remembered Tommy. Oh! How he was like his father, his very image, each day becoming more his likeness. She was so proud.

~ ~ ~

When Thomas graduated college, he applied for admission at the university of medicine in the capitol. His acceptance granted him the distinction of becoming one of the first colored to attend the university, and Myra was overcome with joy. She had always wanted him to achieve his dreams, and she couldn't help but wish that Tommy was here to see him, but she worried about him becoming a minority. She feared what it would mean, and difficult it makes his road to success. Many obstacles still stood in the way of his becoming a doctor. She feared for his failure, but prayed for his success.

The university became an obsession for Thomas. He threw himself into his work, unlike anything he had ever tried. He was destined for success, and showed great promise, as was voiced by his professors. Exactly what field of medicine was undecided, but whatever he chose, she felt comfortable that he would become accomplished. Myra read his letters, and by now she had gotten a telephone in her home, Thomas called her at least twice weekly to keep her posted on what was going on. She baked and mailed him care packages to help keep him going, to support him through the long unforgiving hours he had to endure. She would bake him tea cakes, brownies, and divinity to mail. He always called bragging how wonderful they were, and having to fight to keep them for himself from the other students. He had told her often he had to hide them to keep them from being taken and eaten. She would beam with pride. She baked more and mailed them.

One morning while waiting for class, a secretary approached Thomas telling him she had received a telephone call from the hospital in Greensboro. It was Myra, she was ill, and the doctor, knowing Thomas was in medical school, wanted to talk to him and let him know what was going on. As Thomas called, thoughts ran through his mind, wondering if his mama was all right. Had she had a stroke? Had she fallen? Was she all- right? He was worried, and eager to hear. The doctor answered, advising Thomas that Myra had had a spell with dizziness, and that her blood pressure was rather high. He had examined her in detail, and felt that a few days stay in the clinic was appropriate so he could keep an eye on her. Agreeing, Thomas took note, and asked the doctor if he thought it was a stroke. The doctor was sure at this time it was mostly a warning, but with her elevated blood pressure, he felt with medication and diet, she could work through this. Thomas was eased, but not totally comfortable. Myra was all he had and losing her was not an option. What to do? Should he go home for a few days, or just wait and see? Deciding to stay and continue on at the university, Thomas called his mother, and told her how much he loved her. He told her to mind the doctor and if anything changed to be sure and call him. Myra agreed.

Days turned into weeks, and Myra seemed to regain her strength, and again resumed her household work and responsibilities of working in the café. She never mentioned anything to Thomas about how she was doing, although each time they spoke the conversation always came up, and she would always give the same reply, telling him she was fine, and no recurrences of dizziness. She would tell him she had taken her blood pressure medication and did so faithfully, which she did. Easing Thomas' mind, she would tell him she loved him, and then send him a kiss over the phone, and hang up. Thomas still worried, he was her son, and he loved his mother.

∽ ∽ ∽

Walking into the house one evening after leaving the café, Myra noticed the door to the house was open. Had she forgotten to lock it? She must surely be slipping. It worried her. She walked in, then noticed some things rearranged on the table in the front room. It scared her, was someone in the house? She started backing out the door, when a voice called from within the kitchen? "Are you hungry Mama?" It was Thomas! She cried, and leapt from where she stood into his arms, hugging and kissing him. How happy could one woman be? Almost at the same time, another voice from the kitchen said, "I've made biscuits, grits; we have muscadine jelly, hot coffee, and ham." Myra, backed off, stood, looking at Thomas, and asked, "Well, young man, just who is this in my kitchen?" "Oh, Mama, I want you to meet Sara, a fellow student of mine at the university." Sara was a tall, dark skinned young woman. She was in her early twenties, with dark brown hair, and very pretty. Myra, without saying a word, knew exactly what this meant. Her heart beat fast, and then sank; Thomas was still her son, but no longer her little boy! It was bound to happen. It was a good thing, but it could have waited. Thomas had great things to do, cure to find, people to heal, and romance was not in any prescription she had seen written. But, she smiled gracefully, walking to Sara, and hugging her, and welcoming her in her home. Myra just looked at Sara, and then started laughing, she knew exactly what Sara had on her mind, and there stood Thomas, like a lamb surrounded by wolves. Poor guy, he never knew what hit him and he sure never saw it coming. Oh! Well! She was pretty, and if she was half as sweet and good as she was pretty, he had hit the jackpot. Myra was happy. Deep down in her heart, she felt a gut feeling and became overjoyed, she had already started imagining grandchildren. How awful, they hadn't even mentioned marrying, but they would, she could just feel it. The front room seemed cold mainly because the conversation was of a two way nature rather than a three way. Myra felt like a third wheel, and having excused herself for a bath and getting ready for bed, she eased off and into her room. Before she left, she kissed them both, wished them a good night, made sure she showed Sara where her room was, and reminded Thomas of where his was. With a hint of embarrassment, Thomas acknowledged her advice, and Myra excused herself. Mama was just mama, she would never change!

Myra woke up to the smell of bacon, eggs, biscuits and coffee, her favorite breakfast. It had to be Sara. She knew Thomas couldn't cook! As she gathered her housecoat around her she walked into the kitchen, and there stood Sara at the stove, humming, and turning the eggs. "How do you like your eggs, Miss Myra?" "Cooked, honey", said Myra, then breaking out into a laugh. "You can fry them, sweetie. It's not often I have food cooked for me, so I'll take it anyway I can get it." They both laughed, with Sara saying, "I know what you mean." Sitting at the table, sipping her coffee from a saucer, Myra looked at Thomas, then at Sara." You two sure like a happy couple. I hope it's more than friendship?" Thomas and Sara looked at each other, then at Myra, "Yes mam, it is, and Mama, I would like to ask your permission in my asking Sara to be my wife?" Myra nearly fell out of the chair, almost choking on a biscuit.

"You don't say?" "Yes mam", said Thomas. "I love her, she loves me, we both are studying to become doctors, and each of us feels led to spend our lives together." Myra cried, thinking in her mind, "If only Tommy could be here and hear this." Holding their hands, Myra continued to cry and said, "You have my blessing, and you have my love." Thomas looked at Sara, then to Myra, and both began to feel tears well up in their eyes. They would set the date, and of course Myra would have a front row seat.

~ ~ ~

As Sara walked down the aisle, Myra watched with big tears in her eyes. She kept looking between Thomas and Sara, and watching the smiles on their faces, and the tears in their eyes. It was their day, but also Myra's and Tommy's day. The day they never had, but had always hoped for. As Myra watched Sara gracefully stroll down the aisle she couldn't help but place herself in her shoes, in her mind, and envision Tommy standing there at the altar waiting for her, a dream that was never destined to happen. She felt no remorse, only love. She had had it all, and now, with God's blessing, Thomas would have it all. Sara was an angel, but another angel was looking over him. So far, three angels had come to earth and had kept vigil over him. And, there in the congregation, on the grooms side, with Conrad, sat Miss Jean, wearing her Sunday best, smiling happily, as if yet another angel was still on duty watching the unfolding of a perfect story reach its climax. Conrad, not of angelic demeanor, but yet still kind and considered a "teddy bear", gave way to the glimpse of a smile every now and then.

Vows were exchanged, and promises were made that with God's blessing would be eternal. As the happy couple exited the church, walking out after them, Myra looked up in the sunny sky, smiled, winked and said, "Tommy, we did it!" As Tommy stepped into the car, Miss Jean walked up to him, hugged him and said, "A little something for the road Tommy." Thanking her, and hugging her back, Tommy smiled, waved and threw a kiss at his mother, then closed the door. As the car drove down the road from the church and to the train depot, he felt the letter in his pocket, so reaching inside he removed it. His eyes grew big; he paused for what seemed an eternity, then with trembling hands turned the envelope over and began to open it. As it broke the seal, inside he found a note that read...."Thomas, the angel retires today, off duty, but I've turned you over to newer angel, one who loves you and who will watch over you as did your mother and I. Remember, you are still being watched. Spend it wisely! "It read, Love, Miss Jean and Conrad". Thomas broke down and cried, all these years the letters came, and he never knew who it was, and this lady whom he had known his entire life had been his guardian angel, a white guardian angel. Inside and under the note, there were five crisp new one hundred dollar bills.

~ ~ ~

Myra continued to write and maintain close contact with Thomas and Sara. Although she threw herself once again into her work, she had moments of severe loneliness, soon overcome with the hint of another household project to complete. Her life these days revolved mainly around the café and her home. Never venturing far from home, in the event one of the kids might call her to talk or seek advice.

Meals now amounted to single servings, so the daily housekeeping chores grew less and less. No longer was it a major task, now it was in mostly a maintain mode. Myra continued to actively support her church, and on Sundays she could be found usually, weather permitting, at Greensboro Cemetery placing flowers of the graves of her mother and father and, of course, Tommy. She talked to him as she stood there, sometimes bending over to pull weeds from around the headstone. It was as if she knew with certainty that he heard every word she said, and more like he was real and not dead. She could now tell him everything, all the time. Of course, it brought back memories, but she had learned to get beyond that, at least the part of his being dead. She would never get over missing him, and never planned to. From where she stood at Tommy's grave, she could turn around and look across the fence to her parent's grave. They were practically side by side with not a lot of distance separating them. Each visit, she longed for him more. It was an ache that would never die.

Myra had already begun to think about her passing, not that she was ready, but you never knew when the Lord might call you home, and when he did she certainly wanted her affairs in order. She did not want Thomas or Sara to have to plan anything, rather, she would have it all written down, just as she wished, and she expected it to be followed to the tee. If they didn't like it, tough, that's the way it was!

The cat scratched at the back door, it was time for Myra to feed her. Until now, no pets had ever been allowed to come inside, just something you did not do. But, with the loneliness, and the need for companionship, Myra gave in to the cries in the night, the scratching at the door, and she soon gave in. The cat had chosen her, and Myra could not imagine why. Maybe it was just meant to be. Who knows? At any rate, she had made a bed for it to sleep in the kitchen, near the stove so it would stay warm, and have it a little water bowl and food bowl in the corner near the back door. Regardless of where she put it, the cat always seemed to find its way onto her bed during the night, and when she awakened in the morning she would either be on the pillow beside her or on her feet. It liked rubbing its head on her feet, and with sudden surprise to let Myra know she was hungry, she would snap her head around, and place her teeth right on the top of Myra's feet. Scaring Myra, the cat would bounce off down the hall with its back all hunched up, acting as if it was in serious pursuit of prey, but it was just a game. Myra had come to find humor in the cat and they had developed a strong bond. The cat became accustomed to crawling up in her lap, and lying down to nap. Myra felt accepted, and as she rubbed her the purring just grew louder and louder. Maybe this was her guardian in the absence of Thomas and Tommy. Although Tommy never lived with her, he had still protected her.

She made her way home through the rain and cold carrying several bags of groceries from the corner grocery store. Used to walking, regardless of the weather, Myra felt it was a sure way to prolong her health. After all, she had been walking her entire life, so another few steps wouldn't hurt. Walking in, she took the groceries to the kitchen placing them on the counter to put them away. She hadn't fed the cat, so after several minutes of having to walk around her and nearly tripping on her, Myra made her way to the food bowl, picking it up to wash it and dry it off. "You'd think I was starving you", she said in a joking manner. With its tail in the air sticking straight up, weaved in and out of Myra's legs purring in thanks for her food.

The few items she had picked up would sustain her for quite a while. "Didn't take much for one", she thought as she walked about the kitchen opening and closing cupboard doors. "We need some heat, little girl, what you say?" she said to the cat as she walked past. She turned on the stove, opened the oven door, then sat at the table and waited to gather the energy to begin cooking her supper. "Why do I feel this way", she kept telling herself over and over, I feel funny. Rather than call the clinic, she chose to continue on with her work, cooking supper, and cleaning up afterwards. The radio had been turned on to catch the evening news, but as usual it was so depressing, she chose to turn it off, sit by the stove at the table and read her Bible, which she did. She had several passages of preference, settling on one she felt called to read. Reading her Bible was a pleasant experience and one she felt necessary. It gave her more profound closeness to God, she felt, and since she had done it since childhood, mainly because of her mother, she continued doing it. "God's word makes you a better person", she thought aloud as she read. "It's like another meal all over again, and sometimes you eat so much you could just pop." Myra was a deeply religious woman, having years ago, asked the Lord to forgive her for her sins, and to save her soul. Yes, she was a born again Christian and she let it show. She regularly visited the old folk's home in Greensboro, often to sit and read to those who could not see. For her, it was both a mission of love, and one of fulfillment. It met her needs of companionship, and hopefully, it gave someone else the sense of belonging and being needed.

The circulation in her legs was no longer as it had been. She easily got cramps, caused by poor blood supply, and if she sat for long periods of time in one spot, she arose, to almost fall flat on her face, from both legs being asleep. She realized that she was nearing the time when she could no longer do what she once did, but she wasn't ready right yet to just lie down and die. Not her. Too much left in this old girl. Yes sir!

Letters came regularly from Sara and Thomas. Each word was read with intensity. Myra lived for their letters and telephone calls. They provided her an escape from Greensboro even if it was through the written word or telephone. She loved her kids, as she called them. Sara had surprised her on the telephone by telling her that she was going to be a grandmother. Myra shouted aloud, and yelled, "Praise the Lord, a baby in the house again. She found herself, gathering old pieces of cloth and immediately began quilting a baby quilt. She wanted her baby kept warm. She made booties, little gowns, and all sorts of things, not caring whether it be a boy or girl; it was a baby and it was her grandchild. Her eyes were becoming weakened with age, and it was hard for her to see good enough to sew, but never the less, she still managed to get it done. Nothing would stop this endeavor. She even, began a diary of events in their lives, from things that had happened in her childhood, then on to Thomas, then till present. She made every effort to leave an in depth detailed chronicle of their family lineage. Someday, hopefully, when the baby grew up, he or she would be able to take this diary and from the written words left by Myra, have some idea of who the family really was and how they had all made contributions.

When it came time to write about Thomas, she worried if there would be enough paper. There are some things a parent can not say enough of to a child, and Myra was determined to give this baby something to hold on to. She would even talk about Tommy. After all, he was a part of its blood line, too; an important part. Myra made no bones about Tommy. She loved him She never boasted it, she kept it private, but she did love him. She couldn't help it if the times were like they were, but she prayed for a day when things would be different, to prevent from happening to someone else what had happened to them. She had been given a life of loneliness having loved a man she could only see from a distance, and each feeling the same about each other. She cried again, and always did when she pondered the subject. He was always in her heart.

~ ~ ~

Thomas and Sara had called, and told Myra they would be home this weekend. That gave Myra the necessary two days to scrub, clean, wash, and cook enough ahead to not put too much of a burden on any one of them. She had plans to spend time talking with her daughter-in-law, and son. She would entice them to stay for church, and maybe if the opportunity arose, an evening out, driving the full twenty five miles to Charlesville and eating at the catfish hut. Myra loved eating fish. She especially loved catfish, and better than that, Mississippi Catfish. She couldn't get enough, and the older she got the more intense her taste for it got. She always said, "When I die, not doubt, I'm bound for catfish heaven."

When they arrived, Thomas beamed at his mother through the window of a brand new Ford. This was the first new car, and the first car, period, their family had ever had. She jumped for joy. Thomas was doing well and he bought a new one. The car had been purchased in the capitol city, and it cost a whole two thousand eight hundred dollars. Myra thought, "This is a house!" "Have you lost your mind boy?" She smiled, walked around it, touched it, then sat down in the driver's seat, and breathed in heavy smelling the newness of the vehicle. It was truly a beautiful car. She was overjoyed.

Not long after they got unloaded, Thomas approached his mama and said, "Come on, it's your night out, let's go." "Where we going, son, I'm not ready?" "It's okay Mama, you look fine, just get in and come on, and we got fish to fry." They drove the twenty five miles to Charlesville, and made an evening of it, even taking in a picture show. Myra hadn't seen a picture show since her teen days when she would go to the walk-in theater on Main Street and see the matinees, walking up the stairs to where the coloreds sat. She loved a picture show, it always made her remember things and at times she became saddened by it.

Driving home, Myra began complaining of a headache, that didn't seem to want to go away, so Thomas stopped at the drug store and Myra went in to buy her some "powders", which she believed was a cure-all for just about anything. Having taken the powders, she went back to the car, got into the back seat, holding the coca-cola in her hand, and leaned her head back on the headrest. As Thomas turned out and onto the highway, Myra rose up and said, "I am so happy for you two. God has answered my prayers, and now that he has brought the hopes of a child, we are doubly blessed. I am so proud of you Thomas, and I know Tommy would be too." With having said this, she leaned back again and closed her eyes.

Thomas continued to drive, as he watched in the rear view mirror the image of his beloved mother asleep in the back seat. The twenty five miles back to Greensboro seemed like an eternity, being a two-lane highway, with not so well kept ride of ways. Pulling into town, he slowed down so as not to awaken his mother any earlier than was necessary; she was tired and she needed her rest. Pulling into the driveway, and Sara getting out unlocking the front door, Thomas opened the back door and asked his mama to get out, but there was no response. Thinking she was in a deep sleep, he took his hand and touched her shoulder slightly, attempting to awaken her. Realizing she would not respond, Thomas bent down and looked into the back seat at the face of his mother, and with a tear in his eye, placing his hand on the side of neck to feel for a pulse, finding out there was not one. He yelled into the house for Sara to come quickly. Once they removed her from the car, Thomas carried her in his arms into the house laying her on her bed. He began to put his medical expertise to practice, but soon knew it was to no avail. His dear sweet mother, who had sacrificed so much for him all these years, had passed beyond the portal of life and into eternal rest. Who was he to deprive her of peace and rest with his father? They were now finally together, to never be parted again, regardless of color, regardless of religion or regardless of status. The medical examiner, the local doctor, soon arrived, and pronounced her dead. As he expressed his condolences to Thomas, addressing him as

Doctor, the old doctor patted him on the back and said, "Thomas, Greensboro needs you, we need young blood. Your mother was a wonderful woman, she was a credit to the town, and she will be missed, and I mean that from the heart."

Services were held for Myra in the old style of the African community. She was waked for a week, then in a slow solemn procession carried her to her final resting place atop the knoll in Greensboro Cemetery, placing her casket above the grave located beside her mother and father, and just across from Tommy, separated only by the fence that separated the whites from the coloreds. As the reverend gave her eulogy, Thomas looked back and forth between the graves of his mother and father, thinking that finally at last they were together. She could now hold his hand without fear of being ridiculed, and she could now hug and hold him close, and Tommy could kiss the bride he never had a chance to marry. As Thomas smiled, he looked to the grave of his father, and softly under his breath said, "She's yours now, dad. Take good care of her."

∼ ∼ ∼

The years passed by. Thomas and Sara would drive the trip home to spend weekends at the old home place and let their young son who was now five years old connect with his past and small town life. As he always did, Thomas made the walking vigil to the Greensboro cemetery to visit the graves of his grandparents and his mother and father. His young son would always follow along, toddling as they went, holding his hand, the little boy looking at his father and asking, "Daddy, who buried here?" Tommy picking him up, wiping the dirt and grass from his shoes, would hold him high in his arms and say, "Son, these are the graves of your Great Grandfather and Great Grandmother. This grave, with the big tombstone is the grave of your grandmother Myra, and that grave there, beside her, just beyond the fence, with the same type tombstone is your grandfather, Tommy, my father and mother." Surprised, the little boy mumbled the words grandfather, grandmother, then looking up at his dad asking, "Daddy, where are grandfather and grandmother?" With a smile on his face, and choking back tears, Thomas held his little boy close and said, "They're in heaven son, where cotton grows."

∼ ∼ ∼

Life in Greensboro remains much the same as it did during the time of Tommy and Myra. Thomas, a successful physician, along with his wife, and three children, still visit the old home place regularly and walk the distance to the Greensboro Cemetery to visit the graves of his parents and grandparents. As the years have passed, other little footsteps have followed Thomas' path and they too ask "Who buried here daddy?"

The past is a reminder of who we are, but in no way determines what we become. Against all odds, Thomas arose from the soft plowed cotton fields of Mississippi to become a successful physician, a loving father, and a testimony to the secret love shared by his mother and father, who in death are one, and now at peace, running hand-in-hand through the meadows and by-ways where cotton grows.

Printed in the United States
68532LVS00007B/109-132